PENGUIN POPULAR CLASSICS

MEASURE FOR MEASURE
BY WILLIAM SHAKESPEARE

PENGUIN POPULAR CLASSICS

MEASURE FOR MEASURE

WILLIAM SHAKESPEARE

PENGUIN BOOKS

PENGUIN BOOKS

Published by the Penguin Group
Penguin Books Ltd, 80 Strand, London WC2R ORL, England
Penguin Putnam Inc., 375 Hudson Street, New York, New York 10014, USA
Penguin Books Australia Ltd, Ringwood, Victoria, Australia
Penguin Books Canada Ltd, 10 Alcorn Avenue, Toronto, Ontario, Canada M4V 3B2
Penguin Books India (P) Ltd, 11 Community Centre, Panchsheel Park,
New Delhi – 110 017, India
Penguin Books (NZ) Ltd, Cnr Rosedale and Airborne Roads, Albany, Auckland,
New Zealand
Penguin Books (South Africa) (Pty) Ltd, 24 Sturdee Avenue, Rosebank 2196 South
Africa

Penguin Books Ltd, Registered Offices: 80 Strand, London WC2R ORL, England

www.penguin.com

First published c. 1601–1608
Published in Penguin Popular Classics 1997
Reprinted with line number 2001

5

Printed in England by Cox & Wyman Ltd, Reading, Berkshire

CONTENTS

THE WORKS OF SHAKESPEARE

<table>
<tr><td>APPROXIMATE DATE</td><td colspan="2" align="center">PLAYS</td><td>FIRST PRINTED</td></tr>
</table>

APPROXIMATE DATE	PLAYS		FIRST PRINTED
Before 1594	HENRY VI *three parts*	*Folio*	1623
	RICHARD III		1597
	TITUS ANDRONICUS		1594
	LOVE'S LABOUR'S LOST		1598
	THE TWO GENTLEMEN OF VERONA		*Folio*
	THE COMEDY OF ERRORS		*Folio*
	THE TAMING OF THE SHREW		*Folio*
1594–1597	ROMEO AND JULIET (*pirated* 1597)		1599
	A MIDSUMMER NIGHT'S DREAM		1600
	RICHARD II		1597
	KING JOHN		*Folio*
	THE MERCHANT OF VENICE		1600
1597–1600	HENRY IV *part i*		1598
	HENRY IV *part ii*		1600
	HENRY V (*pirated* 1600)		*Folio*
	MUCH ADO ABOUT NOTHING		1600
	MERRY WIVES OF WINDSOR (*pirated* 1602)		*Folio*
	AS YOU LIKE IT		*Folio*
	JULIUS CÆSAR		*Folio*
	TROYLUS AND CRESSIDA		1609
1601–1608	HAMLET (*pirated* 1603)		1604
	TWELFTH NIGHT		*Folio*
	MEASURE FOR MEASURE		*Folio*
	ALL'S WELL THAT ENDS WELL		*Folio*
	OTHELLO		1622
	LEAR		1608
	MACBETH		*Folio*
	TIMON OF ATHENS		*Folio*
	ANTONY AND CLEOPATRA		*Folio*
	CORIOLANUS		*Folio*
After 1608	PERICLES (*omitted from the Folio*)		1609
	CYMBELINE		*Folio*
	THE WINTER'S TALE		*Folio*
	THE TEMPEST		*Folio*
	HENRY VIII		*Folio*

POEMS

DATES UNKNOWN		
	VENUS AND ADONIS	1593
	THE RAPE OF LUCRECE	1594
	SONNETS }	1609
	A LOVER'S COMPLAINT }	1609
	THE PHŒNIX AND THE TURTLE	1601

WILLIAM SHAKESPEARE

William Shakespeare was born at Stratford upon Avon in April, 1564. He was the third child, and eldest son, of John Shakespeare and Mary Arden. His father was one of the most prosperous men of Stratford, who held in turn the chief offices in the town. His mother was of gentle birth, the daughter of Robert Arden of Wilmcote. In December, 1582, Shakespeare married Ann Hathaway, daughter of a farmer of Shottery, near Stratford; their first child Susanna was baptized on May 6, 1583, and twins, Hamnet and Judith, on February 22, 1585. Little is known of Shakespeare's early life; but it is unlikely that a writer who dramatized such an incomparable range and variety of human kinds and experiences should have spent his early manhood entirely in placid pursuits in a country town. There is one tradition, not universally accepted, that he fled from Stratford because he was in trouble for deer stealing, and had fallen foul of Sir Thomas Lucy, the local magnate; another that he was for some time a schoolmaster.

From 1592 onwards the records are much fuller. In March, 1592, the Lord Strange's players produced a new play at the Rose Theatre called *Harry the Sixth*, which was very successful, and was probably the *First Part of Henry VI*. In the autumn of 1592 Robert Greene, the best known of the professional writers, as he was dying wrote a letter to three fellow writers in which he warned them against the ingratitude of players in general, and in particular against an 'upstart crow' who 'supposes he is as much able to bombast out a blank verse as the best of you: and being an absolute Johannes Factotum is in his own conceit the only

Shake-scene in a country.' This is the first reference to Shakespeare, and the whole passage suggests that Shakespeare had become suddenly famous as a playwright. At this time Shakespeare was brought into touch with Edward Alleyne the great tragedian, and Christopher Marlowe, whose thundering parts of Tamburlaine, the Jew of Malta, and Dr Faustus Alleyne was acting, as well as Hieronimo, the hero of Kyd's *Spanish Tragedy*, the most famous of all Elizabethan plays.

In April, 1593, Shakespeare published his poem *Venus and Adonis*, which was dedicated to the young Earl of Southampton: it was a great and lasting success, and was reprinted nine times in the next few years. In May, 1594, his second poem, *The Rape of Lucrece*, was also dedicated to Southampton.

There was little playing in 1593, for the theatres were shut during a severe outbreak of the plague; but in the autumn of 1594, when the plague ceased, the playing companies were reorganized, and Shakespeare became a sharer in the Lord Chamberlain's company who went to play in the Theatre in Shoreditch. During these months Marlowe and Kyd had died. Shakespeare was thus for a time without a rival. He had already written the three parts of *Henry VI*, *Richard III*, *Titus Andronicus*, *The Two Gentlemen of Verona*, *Love's Labour's Lost*, *The Comedy of Errors*, and *The Taming of the Shrew*. Soon afterwards he wrote the first of his greater plays – *Romeo and Juliet* – and he followed this success in the next three years with *A Midsummer Night's Dream*, *Richard II*, and *The Merchant of Venice*. The two parts of *Henry IV*, introducing Falstaff, the most popular of all his comic characters, were written in 1597–8.

The company left the Theatre in 1597 owing to disputes over a renewal of the ground lease, and went to play at the

Curtain in the same neighbourhood. The disputes continued throughout 1598, and at Christmas the players settled
the matter by demolishing the old Theatre and re-erecting
a new playhouse on the South bank of the Thames, near
Southwark Cathedral. This playhouse was named the
Globe. The expenses of the new building were shared by
the chief members of the Company, including Shakespeare,
who was now a man of some means. In 1596 he had bought
New Place, a large house in the centre of Stratford, for £60,
and through his father purchased a coat-of-arms from the
Heralds, which was the official recognition that he and his
family were gentlefolk.

By the summer of 1598 Shakespeare was recognized as
the greatest of English dramatists. Booksellers were print-
ing his more popular plays, at times even in pirated or stolen
versions, and he received a remarkable tribute from a young
writer named Francis Meres, in his book *Palladis Tamia*. In
a long catalogue of English authors Meres gave Shakespeare
more prominence than any other writer, and mentioned by
name twelve of his plays.

Shortly before the Globe was opened, Shakespeare had
completed the cycle of plays dealing with the whole story
of the Wars of the Roses with *Henry V*. It was followed by
As You Like it, and *Julius Caesar,* the first of the maturer
tragedies. In the next three years he wrote *Troilus and
Cressida, The Merry Wives of Windsor, Hamlet,* and *Twelfth
Night*.

On March 24, 1603, Queen Elizabeth died. The company
had often performed before her, but they found her suc-
cessor a far more enthusiastic patron. One of the first acts
of King James was to take over the company and to pro-
mote them to be his own servants, so that henceforward
they were known as the King's Men. They acted now very

frequently at Court, and prospered accordingly. In the early years of the reign Shakespeare wrote the more sombre comedies, *All's Well that Ends Well*, and *Measure for Measure*, which were followed by *Othello*, *Macbeth*, and *King Lear*. Then he returned to Roman themes with *Antony and Cleopatra* and *Coriolanus*.

Since 1601 Shakespeare had been writing less, and there were now a number of rival dramatists who were introducing new styles of drama, particularly Ben Jonson (whose first successful comedy, *Every Man in his Humour*, was acted by Shakespeare's company in 1598), Chapman, Dekker, Marston, and Beaumont and Fletcher who began to write in 1607. In 1608 the King's Men acquired a second playhouse, an indoor private theatre in the fashionable quarter of the Blackfriars. At private theatres, plays were performed indoors; the prices charged were higher than in the public playhouses, and the audience consequently was more select. Shakespeare seems to have retired from the stage about this time: his name does not occur in the various lists of players after 1607. Henceforward he lived for the most part at Stratford, where he was regarded as one of the most important citizens. He still wrote a few plays, and he tried his hand at the new form of tragi-comedy – a play with tragic incidents but a happy ending – which Beaumont and Fletcher had popularized. He wrote four of these – *Pericles*, *Cymbeline*, *The Winter's Tale*, and *The Tempest*, which was acted at Court in 1611. For the last four years of his life he lived in retirement. His son Hamnet had died in 1596: his two daughters were now married. Shakespeare died at Stratford upon Avon on April 23, 1616, and was buried in the chancel of the church, before the high altar. Shortly afterwards a memorial which still exists, with a portrait bust, was set up on the North wall. His wife survived him.

When Shakespeare died fourteen of his plays had been separately published in Quarto booklets. In 1623 his surviving fellow actors, John Heming and Henry Condell, with the co-operation of a number of printers, published a collected edition of thirty-six plays in one Folio volume, with an engraved portrait, memorial verses by Ben Jonson and others, and an Epistle to the Reader in which Heming and Condell make the interesting note that Shakespeare's 'hand and mind went together, and what he thought, he uttered with that easiness that we have scarce received from him a blot in his papers'.

The plays as printed in the Quartos or the Folio differ considerably from the usual modern text. They are often not divided into scenes, and sometimes not even into acts. Nor are there place-headings at the beginning of each scene, because in the Elizabethan theatre there was no scenery. They are carelessly printed and the spelling is erratic.

THE ELIZABETHAN THEATRE

Although plays of one sort and another had been acted for many generations, no permanent playhouse was erected in England until 1576. In the 1570's the Lord Mayor and Aldermen of the City of London and the players were constantly at variance. As a result James Burbage, then the leader of the great Earl of Leicester's players, decided that he would erect a playhouse outside the jurisdiction of the Lord Mayor, where the players would no longer be hindered by the authorities. Accordingly in 1576 he built the Theatre in Shoreditch, at that time a suburb of London. The experiment was successful, and by 1592 there were two

more playhouses in London, the Curtain (also in Shoreditch), and the Rose on the south bank of the river, near
Southwark Cathedral.

Elizabethan players were accustomed to act on a variety
of stages; in the great hall of a nobleman's house, or one of
the Queen's palaces, in town halls and in yards, as well as
their own theatre.

The public playhouse for which most of Shakespeare's
plays were written was a small and intimate affair. The
outside measurement of the Fortune Theatre, which was
built in 1600 to rival the new Globe, was but eighty feet
square. Playhouses were usually circular or hexagonal, with
three tiers of galleries looking down upon the yard or pit,
which was open to the sky. The stage jutted out into the
yard so that the actors came forward into the midst of their
audience.

Over the stage there was a roof, and on either side doors
by which the characters entered or disappeared. Over the
back of the stage ran a gallery or upper stage which was
used whenever an upper scene was needed, as when Romeo
climbs up to Juliet's bedroom, or the citizens of Angiers
address King John from the walls. The space beneath this
upper stage was known as the tiring house; it was concealed
from the audience by a curtain which could be drawn back
to reveal an inner stage, for such scenes as the witches' cave
in *Macbeth,* Prospero's cell, or Juliet's tomb.

There was no general curtain concealing the whole stage,
so that all scenes on the main stage began with an entrance
and ended with an exit. Thus in tragedies the dead must be
carried away. There was no scenery, and therefore no limit
to the number of scenes, for a scene came to an end when
the characters left the stage. When it was necessary for the
exact locality of a scene to be known, then Shakespeare

THE GLOBE THEATRE
Wood-engraving by R. J. Beedham after a reconstruction by J.C. Adams

indicated it in the dialogue; otherwise a simple property or a garment was sufficient; a chair or stool showed an indoor scene, a man wearing riding boots was a messenger, a king wearing armour was on the battlefield, or the like. Such simplicity was on the whole an advantage; the spectator was not distracted by the setting and Shakespeare was able to use as many scenes as he wished. The action passed by very quickly: a play of 2500 lines of verse could be acted in two hours. Moreover, since the actor was so close to his audience, the slightest subtlety of voice and gesture was easily appreciated.

The company was a 'Fellowship of Players', who were all partners and sharers. There were usually ten to fifteen full members, with three or four boys, and some paid servants. Shakespeare had therefore to write for his team. The chief actor in the company was Richard Burbage, who first distinguished himself as Richard III; for him Shakespeare wrote his great tragic parts. An important member of the company was the clown or low comedian. From 1594 to 1600 the company's clown was Will Kemp; he was succeeded by Robert Armin. No women were allowed to appear on the stage, and all women's parts were taken by boys.

MEASURE FOR MEASURE

The earliest record of *Measure for Measure* is an entry in 'The Accompte of the Office of the Reuelles of the whole yeres Charge in An° 1604 vntell the last of October 1605.' The account notes in three columns the company of players, the date of performance and the play, and the author of each play. The entry reads: *By his Mat^is plaiers | On St Stiuens night* [December 26] *in the Hall A play caled Mesur for Mesur | Shaxberd.* During the months covered by the account the King's Men also played '*The Moor of Venis*', '*the Merry wiues of winsor*', '*the plaie of Errors*', '*A play of Loues Labours Lost*', '*Henry the fift*', '*Euery on out of his vmor*', '*Euery on In his vmor*', '*the Marchant of Venis*', '*the Spanish maz*'. As some of these plays were at least ten years old, the entry gives no more than a latest possible date for the writing of *Measure for Measure*.

Apart from this mention there is no other contemporary record, nor does the play itself contain any certain topical allusion which can be accurately dated. The dislike of Duke Vincentio for the loud applause and 'aves vehement' of his people would have reminded the original spectators of the similar dislike of King James I for the cheers of Londoners, but this trait in his character was noted from the earliest weeks of the new reign. *Measure for Measure* can thus be dated only from the evidence of the style which would seem to place it between *Othello* (c.1602) and *Lear* (1606).

The play was first printed in the first Folio of 1623 where the text has its peculiarities. It contains a number of short lines; several exits and entrances, especially of minor char-

acters who come and go while their betters are speaking,
are omitted; verse is occasionally printed as prose and prose
as verse – an easy mistake at a period when poets were not
accustomed to use a capital letter at the beginning of a line
of verse; and the division of the verse lines is at times not
acceptable to modern editors. As a whole, however, the
Folio text is quite good and offers few serious difficulties of
reading.

The peculiarities of the Folio text are not of great signifi-
cance, nor are they necessarily signs of a corrupt text, nor
do they justify elaborate theories of tampering, revision,
rewriting or collaboration. Shakespeare was always experi-
menting, and in his later plays short lines of verse, and lines
which do not follow the norm of five stresses, are common
and intentional. If *Measure for Measure* was indeed written
in 1604, marked differences of style would not be surpris-
ing. From the early summer of 1603 until the end of 1604
there was no playing in London because of a bad outbreak
of plague. There was therefore no demand for new plays.
Measure for Measure may thus be the first play which
Shakespeare had written for more than a year; and this fact
may well account for some of its peculiarities. Indeed, when
read against the background of the later months of 1604, it
does reflect the mood of the times quite closely.

The nearest parallel to the story of the play in Elizabethan times occurs in a dramatic piece called *Promos and Cassandra* written by George Whetstone and published in 1578.
Four years later Whetstone published a prose version of the
story in a collection called *The Heptameron of Civil Dis-
courses*. The outline of the story is as follows:

In Julio in Hungary, Lord Promos revived an old law by
which incontinence was punished by the death of the man

and the perpetual shame of the woman. As a result a young gentleman called Andrugio was condemned to death. His sister, Cassandra, thereupon petitioned Lord Promos to pardon her brother. Promos was so much delighted with her beauty and conversation that he reprieved Andrugio, but after a while his liking changed to lust and he demanded that she should ransom her brother by sacrificing her honour. Cassandra, won over by her brother's pleading, reluctantly agreed on the condition that Promos should then pardon her brother and marry her. Promos promised to abide by these conditions, but as soon as he had satisfied his will he commanded the jailer to present Cassandra with her brother's head. The jailer, however, befriended Andrugio and instead brought to Cassandra the head of a newly executed felon, and then set Andrugio free. Cassandra thereupon complained to the King, who hastened to do justice on Promos. He commanded that Promos should marry Cassandra and forthwith be beheaded, but no sooner had the marriage been solemnized than Cassandra begged the King to spare her new husband. When the King refused, Andrugio, perceiving the grief of his sister, came forward and at the risk of his own life begged the King to be merciful. The King was so greatly moved that he pardoned Andrugio and Promos.

Although the story in its general details resembles the story of the play, it is likely that some other version, possibly one of the many Elizabethan plays now lost, was the actual source of *Measure for Measure*. But even if Shakespeare took his outline from Whetstone, he added the substitution of Mariana for Isabella, Lucio and the affairs of Pompey from his own imagination, and very considerably altered the details and the motivation of the plot.

The present text, following the principles adopted for the

other volumes of the Penguin Shakespeare, follows the
first Folio closely. Spelling has been modernized, but the
original arrangement and punctuation (which shows how
the speeches should be delivered) have been kept except
where they seemed definitely wrong and likely to cause
confusion. The reader who is used to the 'accepted text'
will thus find some unfamiliarities, but the text itself is
nearer to that used in Shakespeare's own playhouse.

Measure for Measure

THE ACTORS' NAMES

Vincentio, the Duke
Angelo, the Deputy
Escalus, an ancient Lord
Claudio, a young Gentleman
Lucio, a fantastique
2 Other like Gentlemen
Provost
Thomas } 2 Friars
Peter
Elbow, a simple Constable
Froth, a foolish Gentleman
Clown
Abhorson, an Executioner
Barnardine, a dissolute prisoner
Isabella, sister to Claudio
Mariana, betrothed to Angelo
Juliet, beloved of Claudio
Francisca, a Nun
Mistress Over-done, a Bawd

Also
A Justice
Varrius
Boy to Mariana

I. 1

Enter Duke, Escalus, Lords.

DUKE: Escalus.

ESCALUS: My Lord.

DUKE: Of government, the properties to unfold,   5
Would seem in me t' affect speech and discourse,
Since I am put to know, that your own science
Exceeds (in that) the lists of all advice
My strength can give you: Then no more remains,
But that, to your sufficiency, as your worth is able,   10
And let them work: The nature of our People,
Our City's institutions, and the terms
For common justice, you're as pregnant in
As Art, and practice, hath enriched any
That we remember: There is our commission,   15
From which we would not have you warp; call hither,
I say, bid come before us Angelo:
What figure of us think you, he will bear.
For you must know, we have with special soul
Elected him our absence to supply;   20
Lent him our terror, dress'd him with our love,
And given his deputation all the organs
Of our own power: What think you of it?

ESCALUS: If any in Vienna be of worth
To undergo such ample grace, and honour,   25
It is Lord Angelo.

Enter Angelo.

DUKE: Look where he comes.

ANGELO: Always obedient to your Grace's will,
I come to know your pleasure.   30

DUKE: Angelo:
There is a kind of character in thy life,
That to th' observer, doth thy history
Fully unfold: Thyself, and thy belongings
5 Are not thine own so proper, as to waste
Thyself upon thy virtues; they on thee:
Heaven doth with us, as we, with torches do,
Not light them for themselves: For if our virtues
Did not go forth of us, 'twere all alike
10 As if we had them not: Spirits are not finely touch'd,
But to fine issues: nor nature never lends
The smallest scruple of her excellence,
But like a thrifty goddess, she determines
Herself the glory of a creditor,
15 Both thanks, and use; but I do bend my speech
To one that can my part in him advertise;
Hold therefore, Angelo:
In our remove, be thou at full, ourself:
Mortality and mercy in Vienna
20 Live in thy tongue, and heart: Old Escalus
Though first in question, is thy secondary.
Take thy commission.
ANGELO: Now good my Lord
Let there be some more test, made of my metal,
25 Before so noble, and so great a figure
Be stamp'd upon it.
DUKE: No more evasion:
We have with a leaven'd, and prepared choice
Proceeded to you; therefore take your honours:
30 Our haste from hence is of so quick condition,
That it prefers itself, and leaves unquestion'd
Matters of needful value: We shall write to you,
As time, and our concernings shall importune,

How it goes with us, and do look to know
What doth befall you here. So fare you well:
To th' hopeful execution do I leave you,
Of your commissions.

ANGELO: Yet give leave (my Lord,)   5
That we may bring you something on the way.

DUKE: My haste may not admit it,
Nor need you (on mine honour) have to do
With any scruple: your scope is as mine own,
So to inforce, or qualify the Laws   10
As to your soul seems good: Give me your hand,
I'll privily away: I love the people,
But do not like to stage me to their eyes:
Though it do well, I do not relish well
Their loud applause, and Aves vehement: 15
Nor do I think the man of safe discretion
That does affect it. Once more fare you well.

ANGELO: The heavens give safety to your purposes!

ESCALUS: Lead forth, and bring you back in happiness.

DUKE: I thank you, fare you well.   20

Exit.

ESCALUS: I shall desire you, Sir, to give me leave
To have free speech with you; and it concerns me
To look into the bottom of my place:
A power I have, but of what strength and nature,   25
I am not yet instructed.

ANGELO: 'Tis so with me: Let us withdraw together,
And we may soon our satisfaction have
Touching that point.

ESCALUS: I'll wait upon your honour.   30

Exeunt.

I.2

Enter Lucio and two other Gentlemen.

LUCIO: If the Duke, with the other Dukes, come not to composition with the King of Hungary, why then all the Dukes fall upon the King.

1 GENTLEMAN: Heaven grant us its peace, but not the King of Hungary's.

2 GENTLEMAN: Amen.

LUCIO: Thou conclud'st like the sanctimonious pirate, that went to sea with the ten Commandments, but scrap'd one out of the Table.

2 GENTLEMAN: Thou shalt not steal?

LUCIO: Ay, that he raz'd.

1 GENTLEMAN: Why? 'twas a commandment, to command the captain and all the rest from their functions: they put forth to steal: There's not a soldier of us all, that in the thanksgiving before meat, do relish the petition well, that prays for peace.

2 GENTLEMAN: I never heard any soldier dislike it.

LUCIO: I believe thee; for I think thou never wast where grace was said.

2 GENTLEMAN: No? a dozen times at least.

1 GENTLEMAN: What? In metre?

LUCIO: In any proportion, or in any language.

1 GENTLEMAN: I think, or in any religion.

LUCIO: Ay, why not? Grace is grace, despite of all controversy: as, for example; Thou thyself art a wicked villain, despite of all grace.

1 GENTLEMAN: Well: there went but a pair of shears between us.

LUCIO: I grant: as there may between the lists, and the velvet. Thou art the list.

1 GENTLEMAN: And thou the velvet; thou art good velvet; thou'rt a three-pil'd piece I warrant thee: I had as lief be a list of an English kersey, as be pil'd, as thou art pil'd, for a French velvet. Do I speak feelingly now?

LUCIO: I think thou dost: and indeed with most painful 5 feeling of thy speech: I will, out of thine own confession, learn to begin thy health; but, whilst I live forget to drink after thee.

1 GENTLEMAN: I think I have done myself wrong, have I not? 10

2 GENTLEMAN: Yes, that thou hast; whether thou art tainted, or free.

Enter Bawd.

LUCIO: Behold, behold, where Madam Mitigation comes. I have purchas'd as many diseases under her roof, as 15 come to—

2 GENTLEMAN: To what, I pray?

LUCIO: Judge.

2 GENTLEMAN: To three thousand dolours a year.

1 GENTLEMAN: Ay, and more. 20

LUCIO: A French crown more.

1 GENTLEMAN: Thou art always figuring diseases in me; but thou art full of error, I am sound.

LUCIO: Nay, not (as one would say) healthy: but so sound, as things that are hollow; thy bones are hollow; 25 impiety has made a feast of thee.

1 GENTLEMAN: How now, which of your hips has the most profound sciatica?

BAWD: Well, well; there's one yonder arrested, and carried to prison, was worth five thousand of you all. 30

2 GENTLEMAN: Who's that I pray thee?

BAWD: Marry Sir, that's Claudio, Signior Claudio.

1 GENTLEMAN: Claudio to prison? 'tis not so.

BAWD: Nay, but I know 'tis so: I saw him arrested: saw him carried away; and which is more, within these three days his head to be chopp'd off.

LUCIO: But, after all this fooling, I would not have it so:
5   Art thou sure of this?

BAWD: I am too sure of it: and it is for getting Madam Julietta with child.

LUCIO: Believe me this may be: he promis'd to meet me two hours since, and he was ever precise in promise
10   keeping.

2 GENTLEMAN: Besides you know, it draws something near to the speech we had to such a purpose.

1 GENTLEMAN: But most of all agreeing with the proclamation.

15 LUCIO: Away: let's go learn the truth of it.
Exeunt.

BAWD: Thus, what with the war; what with the sweat, what with the gallows, and what with poverty, I am custom-shrunk. How now? what's the news with you?
20   *Enter Clown.*

CLOWN: Yonder man is carried to prison.

BAWD: Well: what has he done?

CLOWN: A woman.

BAWD: But what's his offence?

25 CLOWN: Groping for trouts, in a peculiar river.

BAWD: What? is there a maid with child by him?

CLOWN: No; but there's a woman with maid by him: you have not heard of the proclamation, have you?

BAWD: What proclamation, man?

30 CLOWN: All houses in the Suburbs of Vienna must be pluck'd down.

BAWD: And what shall become of those in the City?

CLOWN: They shall stand for seed: they had gone down

too, but that a wise Burgher put in for them.

BAWD: But shall all our houses of resort in the Suburbs be pull'd down?

CLOWN: To the ground, Mistress.

BAWD: Why here's a change indeed in the Common-   5
wealth: what shall become of me?

CLOWN: Come: fear not you: good counsellors lack no clients: though you change your place, you need not change your trade: I'll be your tapster still; courage; there will be pity taken on you; you that have worn   10
your eyes almost out in the service, you will be considered.

BAWD: What's to do here, Thomas Tapster? let's withdraw.

CLOWN: Here comes Signior Claudio, led by the Provost   15
to prison; and there's Madam Juliet.

Exeunt.

I. 3

Enter Provost, Claudio, Juliet, Officers, Lucio
and two Gentlemen.   20

CLAUDIO: Fellow, why dost thou show me thus to th'
world?

Bear me to prison, where I am committed.

PROVOST: I do it not in evil disposition,

But from Lord Angelo by special charge.   25

CLAUDIO: Thus can the demi-god (Authority)

Make us pay down, for our offence, by weight

The words of heaven: on whom it will, it will;

On whom it will not (so) yet still 'tis just.

LUCIO: Why how now Claudio? whence comes this re-   30
straint?

CLAUDIO: From too much liberty, (my Lucio) liberty
    As surfeit is the father of much fast,
    So every scope by the immoderate use
    Turns to restraint: Our natures do pursue
5   Like rats that ravin down their proper bane,
    A thirsty evil, and when we drink, we die.
LUCIO: If I could speak so wisely under an arrest, I would
    send for certain of my creditors: and yet, to say the
    truth, I had as lief have the foppery of freedom, as the
10   morality of imprisonment: what's thy offence, Claudio?
CLAUDIO: What (but to speak of) would offend again.
LUCIO: What, is 't murder?
CLAUDIO: No.
LUCIO: Lechery?
15 CLAUDIO: Call it so.
PROVOST: Away, Sir, you must go.
CLAUDIO: One word, good friend:
    Lucio, a word with you.
LUCIO: A hundred:
20   If they'll do you any good: Is lechery so look'd after?
CLAUDIO: Thus stands it with me: upon a true contract
    I got possession of Julietta's bed,
    You know the Lady, she is fast my wife,
    Save that we do the denunciation lack
25   Of outward order. This we came not to,
    Only for propagation of a dower
    Remaining in the coffer of her friends,
    From whom we thought it meet to hide our love
    Till time had made them for us. But it chances
30   The stealth of our most mutual entertainment
    With character too gross, is writ on Juliet.
LUCIO: With child, perhaps?
CLAUDIO: Unhappily, even so.

And the new Deputy, now for the Duke,
Whether it be the fault and glimpse of newness,
Or whether that the body public, be
A horse whereon the Governor doth ride,
Who, newly in the seat, that it may know   5
He can command; lets it straight feel the spur:
Whether the tyranny be in his place,
Or in his eminence that fills it up
I stagger in: But this new Governor
Awakes me all the enrolled penalties   10
Which have (like unscour'd armour,) hung by th' wall
So long, that nineteen zodiacs have gone round,
And none of them been worn; and for a name
Now puts the drowsy and neglected Act
Freshly on me: 'tis surely for a name.   15
LUCIO: I warrant it is: And thy head stands so tickle on thy
   shoulders, that a milkmaid, if she be in love, may sigh it
   off: Send after the Duke, and appeal to him.
CLAUDIO: I have done so, but he's not to be found.
   I prithee (Lucio) do me this kind service: 20
   This day, my sister should the cloister enter,
   And there receive her approbation.
   Acquaint her with the danger of my state,
   Implore her, in my voice, that she make friends
   To the strict deputy: bid herself assay him,   25
   I have great hope in that: for in her youth
   There is a prone and speechless dialect,
   Such as move men: beside, she hath prosperous art
   When she will play with reason, and discourse,
   And well she can persuade.   30
LUCIO: I pray she may; as well for the encouragement of
   the like, which else would stand under grievous imposi-
   tion: as for the enjoying of thy life, who I would be

sorry should be thus foolishly lost, at a game of tick-
tack: I'll to her.

CLAUDIO: I thank you good friend Lucio.

LUCIO: Within two hours.

5 CLAUDIO: Come Officer, away.

Exeunt.

I.4

Enter Duke and Friar Thomas.

DUKE: No: holy Father, throw away that thought.

10   Believe not that the dribbling dart of Love
      Can pierce a complete bosom: why I desire thee
      To give me secret harbour, hath a purpose
      More grave, and wrinkled, than the aims and ends
      Of burning youth.

15 FRIAR THOMAS: May your Grace speak of it?

DUKE: My holy Sir, none better knows than you
      How I have ever lov'd the life removed,
      And held in idle price, to haunt assemblies
      Where youth, and cost, and witless bravery keeps.

20   I have delivered to Lord Angelo
      (A man of stricture and firm abstinence)
      My absolute power, and place here in Vienna,
      And he supposes me travel'd to Poland,
      (For so I have strew'd it in the common ear)

25   And so it is receiv'd: Now (pious Sir)
      You will demand of me, why I do this.

FRIAR THOMAS: Gladly, my Lord.

DUKE: We have strict Statutes, and most biting Laws,
      (The needful bits and curbs to headstrong weeds,)

30   Which for this fourteen years, we have let slip,
      Even like an o'ergrown lion in a cave

That goes not out to prey: Now, as fond fathers,
Having bound up the threatning twigs of birch,
Only to stick it in their children's sight,
For terror, not to use, in time the rod
More mock'd, than fear'd: so our decrees,　　5
Dead to infliction, to themselves are dead,
And liberty, plucks Justice by the nose;
The baby beats the nurse, and quite athwart
Goes all decorum.

FRIAR THOMAS: It rested in your Grace　　10
To unloose this tied-up justice when you pleas'd:
And it in you more dreadful would have seem'd
Than in Lord Angelo.

DUKE: I do fear: too dreadful:
Sith 'twas my fault, to give the people scope,　　15
'Twould be my tyranny to strike and gall them,
For what I bid them do: For, we bid this be done
When evil deeds have their permissive pass,
And not the punishment: therefore indeed (my
　　father)　　20
I have on Angelo impos'd the office,
Who may in th' ambush of my name, strike home,
And yet, my nature never in the fight
To do in slander: And to behold his sway
I will, as 'twere a brother of your Order,　　25
Visit both Prince, and people: Therefore I prithee
Supply me with the habit, and instruct me
How I may formally in person bear
Like a true Friar: Moe reasons for this action
At our more leisure, shall I render you;　　30
Only, this one: Lord Angelo is precise,
Stands at a guard with envy: scarce confesses
That his blood flows: or that his appetite

Is more to bread than stone : hence shall we see
If power change purpose, what our seemers be.
Exeunt.

I. 5

5   *Enter Isabella and Francisca, a nun.*
ISABELLA : And have you Nuns no farther privileges?
FRANCISCA : Are not these large enough?
ISABELLA : Yes truly; I speak not as desiring more,
     But rather wishing a more strict restraint
10   Upon the Sisterhood, the Votarists of Saint Clare.
          Lucio within.
LUCIO : Hoa? peace be in this place.
ISABELLA : Who's that which calls?
FRANCISCA : It is a man's voice : gentle Isabella
15   Turn you the key, and know his business of him;
     You may; I may not : you are yet unsworn :
     When you have vow'd, you must not speak with men,
     But in the presence of the Prioress;
     Then if you speak, you must not show your face;
20   Or if you show your face, you must not speak :
     He calls again : I pray you answer him.
ISABELLA : Peace and prosperity : who is 't that calls?
          Enter Lucio.
LUCIO : Hail, virgin (if you be) as those cheek-roses
25   Proclaim you are no less : can you so stead me,
     As bring me to the sight of Isabella,
     A Novice of this place, and the fair sister
     To her unhappy brother Claudio?
ISABELLA : Why her unhappy brother? Let me ask,
30   The rather for I now must make you know
     I am that Isabella, and his sister.

LUCIO: Gentle and fair: your Brother kindly greets you;
   Not to be weary with you; he's in prison.
ISABELLA: Woe me; for what?
LUCIO: For that, which if myself might be his judge,
   He should receive his punishment, in thanks: 5
   He hath got his friend with child.
ISABELLA: Sir, make me not your story.
LUCIO: 'Tis true; I would not, though 'tis my familiar sin,
   With maids to seem the lapwing, and to jest
   Tongue far from heart: play with all virgins so: 10
   I hold you as a thing enskied, and sainted,
   By your renouncement, an immortal spirit
   And to be talk'd with in sincerity,
   As with a Saint.
ISABELLA: You do blaspheme the good, in mocking me.   15
LUCIO: Do not believe it: fewness, and truth; 'tis thus,
   Your brother, and his lover have embrac'd;
   As those that feed, grow full: as blossoming time
   That from the seedness, the bare fallow brings
   To teeming foison: even so her plenteous womb   20
   Expresseth his full tilth, and husbandry.
ISABELLA: Someone with child by him? my cousin Juliet?
LUCIO: Is she your cousin?
ISABELLA: Adoptedly, as school maids change their names
   By vain, though apt affection.   25
LUCIO: She it is.
ISABELLA: Oh, let him marry her.
LUCIO: This is the point.
   The Duke is very strangely gone from hence;
   Bore many gentlemen (myself being one)   30
   In hand, and hope of action: but we do learn,
   By those that know the very nerves of State,
   His givings-out, were of an infinite distance

From his true meant design: upon his place,
(And with full line of his authority)
Governs Lord Angelo: A man, whose blood
Is very snow-broth: one, who never feels
5   The wanton stings, and motions of the sense;
But doth rebate, and blunt his natural edge
With profits of the mind: Study, and fast.
He (to give fear to use, and liberty,
Which have, for long, run-by the hideous law,
10 As mice, by lions) hath pick'd out an act,
Under whose heavy sense, your brother's life
Falls into forfeit: he arrests him on it,
And follows close the rigour of the Statute
To make him an example: all hope is gone,
15 Unless you have the grace, by your fair prayer
To soften Angelo: And that's my pith of business
'Twixt you, and your poor brother.
ISABELLA: Doth he so,
Seek his life?
20 LUCIO: Has censur'd him already,
And as I hear, the Provost hath a warrant
For's execution.
ISABELLA: Alas: what poor
Ability's in me, to do him good.
25 LUCIO: Assay the power you have.
ISABELLA: My power? alas, I doubt.
LUCIO: Our doubts are traitors
And make us lose the good we oft might win,
By fearing to attempt: Go to Lord Angelo
30 And let him learn to know, when maidens sue
Men give like gods: but when they weep and kneel,
All their petitions, are as freely theirs
As they themselves would owe them.

ISABELLA: I'll see what I can do.

LUCIO: But speedily.

ISABELLA: I will about it straight;
    No longer staying, but to give the Mother
    Notice of my affair: I humbly thank you: 5
    Commend me to my brother: soon at night
    I'll send him certain word of my success.

LUCIO: I take my leave of you.

ISABELLA: Good sir, adieu.

                Exeunt.   10

II. 1

Enter Angelo, Escalus, Servants, Justice.

ANGELO: We must not make a scarecrow of the Law,
    Setting it up to fear the birds of prey,
    And let it keep one shape, till custom make it   15
    Their perch, and not their terror.

ESCALUS: Ay, but yet
    Let us be keen, and rather cut a little
    Than fall, and bruise to death: alas, this gentleman
    Whom I would save, had a most noble father,   20
    Let but your honour know
    (Whom I believe to be most strait in virtue)
    That in the working of your own affections,
    Had time coher'd with place, or place with wishing,
    Or that the resolute acting of your blood   25
    Could have attain'd th' effect of your own purpose,
    Whether you had not sometime in your life
    Err'd in this point, which now you censure him,
    And pull'd the Law upon you.

ANGELO: 'Tis one thing to be tempted (Escalus)   30
    Another thing to fall: I not deny

The jury passing on the prisoner's life
May in the sworn twelve have a thief, or two
Guiltier than him they try; what's open made to Justice,
That Justice seizes; What knows the Laws
5 That thieves do pass on thieves? 'Tis very pregnant,
The jewel that we find, we stoop, and take't,
Because we see it; but what we do not see,
We tread upon, and never think of it.
You may not so extenuate his offence,
10 For I have had such faults; but rather tell me
When I, that censure him, do so offend,
Let mine own judgement pattern out my death,
And nothing come in partial. Sir, he must die.

Enter Provost.

15 ESCALUS: Be it as your wisdom will.
ANGELO: Where is the Provost?
PROVOST: Here if it like your honour.
ANGELO: See that Claudio
Be executed by nine tomorrow morning.
20 Bring him his Confessor, let him be prepar'd,
For that's the utmost of his pilgrimage.

Exit Provost.

ESCALUS: Well: heaven forgive him; and forgive us all:
Some rise by sin, and some by virtue fall:
25 Some run from brakes of ice, and answer none,
And some condemned for a fault alone.

Enter Elbow, Froth, Clown, Officers.

ELBOW: Come, bring them away: if these be good people
in a Commonweal, that do nothing but use their abuses
30 in common houses, I know no law: bring them away.
ANGELO: How now Sir; what's your name? And what's
the matter?
ELBOW: If it please your honour, I am the poor Duke's

Constable, and my name is Elbow; I do lean upon Justice Sir, and do bring in here before your good honour, two notorious benefactors.

ANGELO: Benefactors? Well: What benefactors are they? Are they not malefactors? 5

ELBOW: If it please your honour, I know not well what they are: But precise villains they are, that I am sure of, and void of all profanation in the world, that good Christians ought to have.

ESCALUS: This comes off well: here's a wise Officer. 10

ANGELO: Go to: What quality are they of? Elbow is your name?

Why dost thou not speak, Elbow?

CLOWN: He cannot Sir; he's out at elbow.

ANGELO: What are you Sir? 15

ELBOW: He Sir: a tapster Sir: parcel bawd: one that serves a bad woman: whose house Sir, was (as they say) pluck'd down in the Suburbs: and now she professes a hot-house; which, I think is a very ill house too.

ESCALUS: How know you that? 20

ELBOW: My wife Sir, whom I detest before heaven, and your honour.

ESCALUS: How? thy wife?

ELBOW: Ay Sir: whom I thank heaven is an honest woman.

ESCALUS: Dost thou detest her therefore? 25

ELBOW: I say sir, I will detest myself also, as well as she, that this house, if it be not a bawd's house, it is pity of her life, for it is a naughty house.

ESCALUS: How dost thou know that, Constable?

ELBOW: Marry sir, by my wife, who, if she had been a 30 woman cardinally given, might have been accus'd in fornication, adultery, and all uncleanliness there.

ESCALUS: By the woman's means?

ELBOW: Ay Sir, by Mistress Overdone's means: but as she
spit in his face, so she defied him.

CLOWN: Sir, if it please your honour, this is not so.

ELBOW: Prove it before these varlets here, thou honour-
5 able man, prove it.

ESCALUS: Do you hear how he misplaces?

CLOWN: Sir, she came in great with child: and longing
(saving your honour's reverence) for stew'd prewins;
sir, we had but two in the house, which at that very dis-
10 tant time stood, as it were in a fruit dish (a dish of some
threepence; your honours have seen such dishes) they
are not China dishes, but very good dishes.

ESCALUS: Go to; go to: no matter for the dish sir.

CLOWN: No indeed sir not of a pin; you are therein in the
15 right: but, to the point: As I say, this Mistress Elbow,
being (as I said) with child, and being great bellied, and
longing (as I said) for prewins: and having but two in
the dish (as I said) Master Froth here, this very man,
having eaten the rest (as I said) and (as I say) paying for
20 them very honestly: for, as you know Master Froth, I
could not give you threepence again.

FROTH: No indeed.

CLOWN: Very well: you being then (if you be remember'd) cracking the stones of the foresaid prewins.

25 FROTH: Ay, so I did indeed.

CLOWN: Why, very well: I telling you then (if you be
remember'd) that such a one, and such a one, were past
cure of the thing you wot of, unless they kept very good
diet, as I told you.

30 FROTH: All this is true.

CLOWN: Why very well then.

ESCALUS: Come: you are a tedious fool: to the purpose:
what was done to Elbow's wife, that he hath cause to

complain of? Come me to what was done to her.

CLOWN: Sir, your honour cannot come to that yet.

ESCALUS: No sir, nor I mean it not.

CLOWN: Sir, but you shall come to it, by your honour's leave: And I beseech you, look into Master Froth here 5 sir, a man of four-score pound a year; whose father died at Hallowmas: Was't not at Hallowmas Master Froth?

FROTH: Allhallond-Eve.

CLOWN: Why very well: I hope here be truths: he Sir, sitting (as I say) in a lower chair, Sir, 'twas in the Bunch 10 of Grapes, where indeed you have a delight to sit, have you not?

FROTH: I have so, because it is an open room, and good for winter.

CLOWN: Why very well then: I hope here be truths. 15

ANGELO: This will last out a night in Russia
When nights are longest there: I'll take my leave,
And leave you to the hearing of the cause;
Hoping you'll find good cause to whip them all.

Exit. 20

ESCALUS: I think no less: good morrow to your Lordship. Now Sir, come on: What was done to Elbow's wife, once more?

CLOWN: Once Sir? there was nothing done to her once.

ELBOW: I beseech you Sir, ask him what this man did to 25 my wife.

CLOWN: I beseech your honour, ask me.

ESCALUS: Well sir, what did this gentleman to her?

CLOWN: I beseech you sir, look in this gentleman's face: good Master Froth look upon his honour: 'tis for a good 30 purpose: doth your honour mark his face?

ESCALUS: Ay sir, very well.

CLOWN: Nay, I beseech you mark it well.

ESCALUS: Well, I do so.

CLOWN: Doth your honour see any harm in his face?

ESCALUS: Why no.

CLOWN: I'll be suppos'd upon a book, his face is the worst
5   thing about him: good then: if his face be the worst
    thing about him, how could Master Froth do the Con-
    stable's wife any harm? I would know that of your
    honour.

ESCALUS: He's in the right (Constable) what say you to
10   it?

ELBOW: First, and it like you, the house is a respected
    house; next, this is a respected fellow; and his Mistress is
    a respected woman.

CLOWN: By this hand Sir, his wife is a more respected per-
15   son than any of us all.

ELBOW: Varlet, thou liest; thou liest wicked varlet; the
    time is yet to come that she was ever respected with man,
    woman, or child.

CLOWN: Sir, she was respected with him, before he
20   married with her.

ESCALUS: Which is the wiser here; Justice or Iniquity? Is
    this true?

ELBOW: O thou caitiff: O thou varlet: O thou wicked
    Hannibal; I respected with her, before I was married to
25   her? If ever I was respected with her, or she with me, let
    not your worship think me the poor Duke's Officer:
    prove this, thou wicked Hannibal, or I'll have mine
    action of battery on thee.

ESCALUS: If he took you a box o' th' ear, you might have
30   your action of slander too.

ELBOW: Marry I thank your good worship for it: what
    is't your Worship's pleasure I shall do with this wicked
    caitiff?

ESCALUS: Truly Officer, because he hath some offences in him, that thou wouldst discover, if thou couldst, let him continue in his courses, till thou knowst what they are.

ELBOW: Marry I thank your worship for it: Thou seest thou wicked varlet now, what's come upon thee. Thou art to continue now thou varlet, thou art to continue.

ESCALUS: Where were you born, friend?

FROTH: Here in Vienna, Sir.

ESCALUS: Are you of fourscore pounds a year?

FROTH: Yes, and't please you sir.

ESCALUS: So: what trade are you of, sir?

CLOWN: A tapster, a poor widow's tapster.

ESCALUS: Your mistress' name?

CLOWN: Mistress Overdone.

ESCALUS: Hath she had any more than one husband?

CLOWN: Nine, sir; Overdone by the last.

ESCALUS: Nine? come hither to me, Master Froth; Master Froth, I would not have you acquainted with tapsters; they will draw you Master Froth, and you will hang them: get you gone, and let me hear no more of you.

FROTH: I thank your worship: for mine own part, I never come into any room in a tap-house, but I am drawn in.

ESCALUS: Well: no more of it Master Froth: farewell:
Exit Froth.

Come you hither to me, Master Tapster: what's your name, Master Tapster?

CLOWN: Pompey.

ESCALUS: What else?

CLOWN: Bum, sir.

ESCALUS: Troth, and your bum is the greatest thing

about you, so that in the beastliest sense, you are Pompey
the Great; Pompey, you are partly a bawd, Pompey;
howsoever you colour it in being a tapster, are you not?
come, tell me true, it shall be the better for you.

5 CLOWN: Truly sir, I am a poor fellow that would live.

ESCALUS: How would you live Pompey? by being a
bawd? what do you think of the trade Pompey? is it a
lawful trade?

CLOWN: If the Law would allow it, sir.

10 ESCALUS: But the Law will not allow it Pompey; nor it
shall not be allowed in Vienna.

CLOWN: Does your Worship mean to geld and splay all
the youth of the city?

ESCALUS: No, Pompey.

15 CLOWN: Truly Sir, in my poor opinion they will to't
then: if your Worship will take order for the drabs and
the knaves, you need not to fear the bawds.

ESCALUS: There is pretty orders beginning I can tell you:
It is but heading, and hanging.

20 CLOWN: If you head, and hang all that offend that way
but for ten year together, you'll be glad to give out a
commission for more heads: if this law hold in Vienna
ten year, I'll rent the fairest house in it after threepence a
bay: if you live to see this come to pass, say Pompey told

25 you so.

ESCALUS: Thank you good Pompey; and in requital
of your prophecy, hark you: I advise you let me not find
you before me again upon any complaint whatsoever:
no, not for dwelling where you do: if I do Pompey, I

30 shall beat you to your tent, and prove a shrewd Caesar to
you: in plain dealing Pompey, I shall have you whipp'd;
so for this time, Pompey, fare you well.

CLOWN: I thank your Worship for your good counsel;

but I shall follow it as the flesh and fortune shall better determine.

Whip me? no, no, let carman whip his jade,
The valiant heart's not whipp'd out of his trade.

Exit.

5

ESCALUS: Come hither to me, Master Elbow: come hither, Master Constable: how long have you been in this place of Constable?

ELBOW: Seven year, and a half, sir.

ESCALUS: I thought by your readiness in the office, you had continued in it some time: you say seven years together?

ELBOW: And a half sir.

ESCALUS: Alas, it hath been great pains to you: they do you wrong to put you so oft upon 't. Are there not men in your Ward sufficient to serve it?

ELBOW: Faith sir, few of any wit in such matters: as they are chosen, they are glad to choose me for them; I do it for some piece of money, and go through with all.

ESCALUS: Look you bring me in the names of some six or seven, the most sufficient of your parish.

ELBOW: To your Worship's house sir?

ESCALUS: To my house: fare you well:

Exit Elbow.

what's o'clock, think you?

25

JUSTICE: Eleven, sir.

ESCALUS: I pray you home to dinner with me.

JUSTICE: I humbly thank you.

ESCALUS: It grieves me for the death of Claudio
But there's no remedy.

30

JUSTICE: Lord Angelo is severe.

ESCALUS: It is but needful.
Mercy is not itself, that oft looks so,

Pardon is still the nurse of second woe:
But yet, poor Claudio; there is no remedy.
Come Sir.

Exeunt.

II. 2

Enter Provost, Servant.

SERVANT: He's hearing of a cause; he will come straight,
I'll tell him of you.
PROVOST: Pray you do. I'll know

Exit Servant.

His pleasure, maybe he will relent; alas
He hath but as offended in a dream,
All sects, all ages smack of this vice, and he
To die for 't?

Enter Angelo.

ANGELO: Now, what's the matter Provost?
PROVOST: Is it your will Claudio shall die tomorrow?
ANGELO: Did not I tell thee yea? hadst thou not order?
Why dost thou ask again?
PROVOST: Lest I might be too rash:
Under your good correction, I have seen
When after execution, Judgement hath
Repented o'er his doom.
ANGELO: Go to; let that be mine,
Do you your office, or give up your place,
And you shall well be spar'd.
PROVOST: I crave your Honour's pardon:
What shall be done Sir, with the groaning Juliet?
She's very near her hour.
ANGELO: Dispose of her
To some more fitter place; and that with speed.

Enter Servant.

SERVANT: Here is the sister of the man condemn'd,
Desires access to you.

ANGELO: Hath he a sister?

PROVOST: Ay my good Lord, a very virtuous maid,   5
And to be shortly of a Sisterhood,
If not already.

ANGELO: Well: let her be admitted;
See you the fornicatress be remov'd,
Let her have needful, but not lavish means,   10
There shall be order for 't.

Enter Lucio and Isabella.

PROVOST: 'Save your Honour.

ANGELO: Stay a little while: You're welcome: what's
your will?   15

ISABELLA: I am a woeful suitor to your Honour,
Please but your Honour hear me.

ANGELO: Well: what's your suit?

ISABELLA: There is a vice that most I do abhor,
And most desire should meet the blow of Justice;   20
For which I would not plead, but that I must,
For which I must not plead, but that I am
At war, 'twixt will, and will not.

ANGELO: Well: the matter?

ISABELLA: I have a brother is condemn'd to die,   25
I do beseech you let it be his fault,
And not my brother.

PROVOST: Heaven give thee moving graces.

ANGELO: Condemn the fault, and not the actor of it,
Why every fault's condemn'd ere it be done: 30
Mine were the very cipher of a function
To fine the faults, whose fine stands in record,
And let go by the actor.

ISABELLA: Oh just, but severe Law:
I had a brother then; heaven keep your honour.
LUCIO: Give 't not o'er so: to him again, entreat him,
Kneel down before him, hang upon his gown,
5 You are too cold: if you should need a pin,
You could not with more tame a tongue desire it:
To him, I say.
ISABELLA: Must he needs die?
ANGELO: Maiden, no remedy.
10 ISABELLA: Yes: I do think that you might pardon him,
And neither heaven, nor man grieve at the mercy.
ANGELO: I will not do 't.
ISABELLA: But can you if you would?
ANGELO: Look what I will not, that I cannot do.
15 ISABELLA: But might you do 't and do the world no wrong
If so your heart were touch'd with that remorse,
As mine is to him?
ANGELO: He's sentenc'd, 'tis too late.
LUCIO: You are too cold.
20 ISABELLA: Too late? why no: I that do speak a word
May call it back again: well, believe this
No ceremony that to great ones 'longs,
Not the King's crown; nor the deputed sword,
The Marshal's truncheon, nor the Judge's robe
25 Become them with one half so good a grace
As mercy does: If he had been as you, and you as he,
You would have slipp'd like him, but he like you
Would not have been so stern.
ANGELO: Pray you be gone.
30 ISABELLA: I would to heaven I had your potency,
And you were Isabel: should it then be thus?
No: I would tell what 'twere to be a Judge,
And what a prisoner.

LUCIO: Ay, touch him: there's the vein.

ANGELO: Your brother is a forfeit of the Law,
And you but waste your words.

ISABELLA: Alas, alas:
Why all the souls that were, were forfeit once,   5
And he that might the vantage best have took,
Found out the remedy: how would you be,
If he, which is the top of judgement, should
But judge you, as you are? Oh, think on that,
And mercy then will breathe within your lips   10
Like man new made.

ANGELO: Be you content, (fair maid)
It is the Law, not I, condemn your brother.
Were he my kinsman, brother, or my son,
It should be thus with him: he must die tomorrow.   15

ISABELLA: Tomorrow? oh, that's sudden,
Spare him, spare him:
He's not prepar'd for death: even for our kitchens
We kill the fowl of season: shall we serve heaven
With less respect than we do minister   20
To our gross selves? good, good my Lord, bethink you;
Who is it that hath died for this offence?
There's many have committed it.

LUCIO: Ay, well said.

ANGELO: The Law hath not been dead, though it hath   25
slept.
Those many had not dar'd to do that evil
If the first, that did th' Edict infringe
Had answer'd for his deed. Now 'tis awake,
Takes note of what is done, and like a Prophet,   30
Looks in a glass that shows what future evils
Either now, or by remissness, new conceiv'd,
And so in progress to be hatch'd, and born,

Are now to have no successive degrees,
But here they live to end.
ISABELLA: Yet show some pity.
ANGELO: I show it most of all, when I show justice;
5   For then I pity those I do not know,
Which a dismiss'd offence, would after gall
And do him right, that answering one foul wrong
Lives not to act another. Be satisfied;
Your brother dies tomorrow; be content.
10 ISABELLA: So you must be the first that gives his sentence,
And he, that suffers: Oh, it is excellent
To have a Giant's strength: but it is tyrannous
To use it like a Giant.
LUCIO: That's well said.
15 ISABELLA: Could great men thunder
As Jove himself does, Jove would ne'er be quiet,
For every pelting, petty Officer
Would use his heaven for thunder;
Nothing but thunder: Merciful heaven,
20   Thou rather with thy sharp and sulphurous bolt
Split'st the unwedgeable and gnarled oak,
Than the soft myrtle: But man, proud man,
Dress'd in a little brief authority,
Most ignorant of what he's most assur'd,
25   (His glassy essence) like an angry ape
Plays such fantastic tricks before high heaven,
As make the angels weep: who with our spleens,
Would all themselves laugh mortal.
LUCIO: Oh, to him, to him wench: he will relent,
30   He's coming: I perceive 't.
PROVOST: Pray Heaven she win him.
ISABELLA: We cannot weigh our brother with ourself,
Great men may jest with Saints: 'tis wit in them,

But in the less foul profanation.
LUCIO: Thou'rt i' th' right (girl) more o' that.
ISABELLA: That in the captain's but a choleric word,
  Which in the soldier is flat blasphemy.
LUCIO: Art avis'd o' that? more on't.   5
ANGELO: Why do you put these sayings upon me?
ISABELLA: Because Authority, though it err like others,
  Hath yet a kind of medicine in itself
  That skins the vice o' th' top; go to your bosom,
  Knock there, and ask your heart what it doth know   10
  That's like my brother's fault: if it confess
  A natural guiltiness, such as is his,
  Let it not sound a thought upon your tongue
  Against my brother's life.
ANGELO: She speaks, and 'tis such sense   15
  That my sense breeds with it; fare you well.
ISABELLA: Gentle my Lord, turn back.
ANGELO: I will bethink me: come again tomorrow.
ISABELLA: Hark, how I'll bribe you: good my Lord turn
  back.   20
ANGELO: How? bribe me?
ISABELLA: Ay, with such gifts that heaven shall share with
  you.
LUCIO: You had marr'd all else.
ISABELLA: Not with fond sicles of the tested gold,   25
  Or stones, whose rates are either rich, or poor
  As fancy values them: but with true prayers,
  That shall be up at heaven, and enter there
  Ere sunrise: prayers from preserved souls,
  From fasting maids, whose minds are dedicate   30
  To nothing temporal.
ANGELO: Well: come to me tomorrow.
LUCIO: Go to: 'tis well; away.

ISABELLA: Heaven keep your honour safe.
ANGELO: Amen.
　　For I am that way going to temptation
　　Where prayers cross.
5 ISABELLA: At what hour tomorrow,
　　Shall I attend your Lordship?
ANGELO: At any time 'fore-noon.
ISABELLA: 'Save your Honour.
　　　　　　Exeunt Isabella, Lucio, and Provost.
10 ANGELO: From thee: even from thy virtue.
　　What's this? what's this? is this her fault, or mine?
　　The tempter, or the tempted, who sins most? ha?
　　Not she: nor doth she tempt: but it is I,
　　That, lying by the violet in the sun,
15 　Do as the carrion does, not as the flower,
　　Corrupt with virtuous season: Can it be,
　　That modesty may more betray our sense
　　Than woman's lightness? having waste ground enough,
　　Shall we desire to raze the Sanctuary
20 　And pitch our evils there? oh fie, fie, fie:
　　What dost thou? or what art thou Angelo?
　　Dost thou desire her foully, for those things
　　That make her good? oh, let her brother live:
　　Thieves for their robbery have authority,
25 　When Judges steal themselves: what, do I love her,
　　That I desire to hear her speak again?
　　And feast upon her eyes? what is't I dream on?
　　O cunning enemy, that to catch a Saint,
　　With Saints dost bait thy hook: most dangerous
30 　Is that temptation, that doth goad us on
　　To sin, in loving virtue: never could the strumpet
　　With all her double vigour, art, and nature
　　Once stir my temper; but this virtuous maid

Subdues me quite: Ever till now
When men were fond, I smil'd, and wonder'd how.
                   Exit.

II. 3

5
                Enter Duke (as a Friar) and Provost.

DUKE: Hail to you, Provost, so I think you are.
PROVOST: I am the Provost: what's your will, good Friar?
DUKE: Bound by my charity, and my blest order,
  I come to visit the afflicted spirits
  Here in the prison: do me the common right   10
  To let me see them; and to make me know
  The nature of their crimes, that I may minister
  To them accordingly.
PROVOST: I would do more than that, if more were needful.
            .   *Enter Juliet.*   15
  Look here comes one: a gentlewoman of mine,
  Who falling in the flaws of her own youth,
  Hath blister'd her report: She is with child,
  And he that got it, sentenc'd: a young man,
  More fit to do another such offence,   20
  Than die for this.
DUKE: When must he die?
PROVOST: As I do think tomorrow.
  I have provided for you, stay awhile,
  And you shall be conducted.   25
DUKE: Repent you (fair one) of the sin you carry?
JULIET: I do; and bear the shame most patiently.
DUKE: I'll teach you how you shall arraign your con-
    science
  And try your penitence, if it be sound,   30
  Or hollowly put on.

JULIET: I'll gladly learn.

DUKE: Love you the man that wrong'd you?

JULIET: Yes, as I love the woman that wrong'd him.

DUKE: So then it seems your most offenceful act
5   Was mutually committed?

JULIET: Mutually.

DUKE: Then was your sin of heavier kind than his.

JULIET: I do confess it, and repent it (Father).

DUKE: 'Tis meet so (daughter) but lest you do repent
10   As that the sin hath brought you to this shame,
    Which sorrow is always toward ourselves, not heaven,
    Showing we would not spare heaven, as we love it,
    But as we stand in fear.

JULIET: I do repent me, as it is an evil,
15   And take the shame with joy.

DUKE: There rest:
    Your partner (as I hear) must die tomorrow,
    And I am going with instruction to him:
    Grace go with you, *Benedicite*.
20   *Exit.*

JULIET: Must die tomorrow? oh injurious Love
    That respites me a life, whose very comfort
    Is still a dying horror.

PROVOST: 'Tis pity of him.
25   *Exeunt.*

II.4

Enter Angelo.

ANGELO: When I would pray, and think, I think, and pray
    To several subjects: heaven hath my empty words,
30   Whilst my invention, hearing not my tongue,
    Anchors on Isabel: heaven in my mouth,

As if I did but only chew his name,
And in my heart the strong and swelling evil
Of my conception: the state whereon I studied
Is like a good thing, being often read
Grown fear'd, and tedious: yea, my gravity   5
Wherein (let no man hear me) I take pride,
Could I, with boot, change for an idle plume
Which the air beats for vain: oh place, oh form,
How often dost thou with thy case, thy habit
Wrench awe from fools, and tie the wiser souls   10
To thy false seeming? Blood, thou art blood.
Let's write good Angel on the Devil's horn
'Tis not the Devil's crest: how now? who's there?

Enter Servant.

SERVANT: One Isabel, a Sister, desires access to you.   15
ANGELO: Teach her the way: oh, heavens
Why does my blood thus muster to my heart,
Making both it unable for itself,
And dispossessing all my other parts
Of necessary fitness?   20
So play the foolish throngs with one that swounds,
Come all to help him, and so stop the air
By which he should revive: and even so
The general subject to a well-wish'd King
Quit their own part, and in obsequious fondness   25
Crowd to his presence, where their untaught love
Must needs appear offence: how now fair maid.

Enter Isabella.

ISABELLA: I am come to know your pleasure.
ANGELO: That you might know it, would much better   30
   please me,
Than to demand what 'tis: your brother cannot live.
ISABELLA: Even so: heaven keep your Honour.

ANGELO: Yet may he live a while; and it may be
    As long as you, or I: yet he must die.
ISABELLA: Under your sentence?
ANGELO: Yea.
5 ISABELLA: When, I beseech you: that in his reprieve
    (Longer, or shorter) he may be so fitted
    That his soul sicken not.
ANGELO: Ha? fie, these filthy vices: It were as good
    To pardon him, that hath from nature stolen
10   A man already made, as to remit
    Their saucy sweetness, that do coin heaven's image
    In stamps that are forbid: 'tis all as easy,
    Falsely to take away a life true made,
    As to put metal in restrained means
15   To make a false one.
ISABELLA: 'Tis set down so in heaven, but not in earth.
ANGELO: Say you so: then I shall pose you quickly.
    Which had you rather, that the most just Law
    Now took your brother's life, and to redeem him,
20   Give up your body to such sweet uncleanness
    As she that he hath stain'd?
ISABELLA: Sir, believe this.
    I had rather give my body, than my soul.
ANGELO: I talk not of your soul: our compell'd sins
25   Stand more for number, than for accompt.
ISABELLA: How say you?
ANGELO: Nay I'll not warrant that: for I can speak
    Against the thing I say: Answer to this,
    I (now the voice of the recorded Law)
30   Pronounce a sentence on your brother's life,
    Might there not be a charity in sin,
    To save this brother's life?
ISABELLA: Please you to do't,

I'll take it as a peril to my soul,
It is no sin at all, but charity.

ANGELO: Pleas'd you to do't, at peril of your soul
Were equal poise of sin, and charity.

ISABELLA: That I do beg his life, if it be sin   5
Heaven let me bear it: you granting of my suit,
If that be sin, I'll make it my morn prayer,
To have it added to the faults of mine,
And nothing of your answer.

ANGELO: Nay, but hear me.   10
Your sense pursues not mine: either you are ignorant,
Or seem so crafty; and that's not good.

ISABELLA: Let me be ignorant, and in nothing good,
But graciously to know I am no better.

ANGELO: Thus wisdom wishes to appear most bright,   15
When it doth tax itself: As these black masks
Proclaim an enshield beauty ten times louder
Than beauty could display'd: But mark me,
To be received plain, I'll speak more gross:
Your brother is to die.   20

ISABELLA: So.

ANGELO: And his offence is so, as it appears,
Accountant to the Law, upon that pain.

ISABELLA: True.

ANGELO: Admit no other way to save his life   25
(As I subscribe not that, nor any other,
But in the loss of question) that you, his sister,
Finding yourself desir'd of such a person,
Whose credit with the Judge, or own great place,
Could fetch your brother from the manacles   30
Of the all-building Law: and that there were
No earthly mean to save him, but that either
You must lay down the treasures of your body,

     To this supposed, or else to let him suffer:
     What would you do?

ISABELLA: As much for my poor brother, as myself;
     That is: were I under the terms of death,
5   Th' impression of keen whips, I'd wear as rubies,
     And strip myself to death, as to a bed,
     That longing have been sick for, ere I'd yield
     My body up to shame.

ANGELO: Then must your brother die.

10 ISABELLA: And 'twere the cheaper way:
     Better it were a brother died at once,
     Than that a sister, by redeeming him
     Should die forever.

ANGELO: Were not you then as cruel as the sentence,
15   That you have slander'd so?

ISABELLA: Ignomy in ransom and free pardon
     Are of two houses: lawful mercy,
     Is nothing kin to foul redemption.

ANGELO: You seem'd of late to make the Law a tyrant,
20   And rather prov'd the sliding of your brother
     A merriment, than a vice.

ISABELLA: Oh pardon me my Lord, It oft falls out
     To have, what we would have,
     We speak not what we mean;
25   I something do excuse the thing I hate,
     For his advantage that I dearly love.

ANGELO: We are all frail.

ISABELLA: Else let my brother die,
     If not a feodary but only he
30   Owe, and succeed thy weakness.

ANGELO: Nay, women are frail too.

ISABELLA: Ay, as the glasses where they view themselves,
     Which are as easy broke as they make forms:

Women? Help heaven; men their creation mar
In profiting by them: Nay, call us ten times frail,
For we are soft, as our complexions are,
And credulous to false prints.
ANGELO: I think it well: 5
And from this testimony of your own sex
(Since I suppose, we are made to be no stronger
Than faults may shake our frames) let me be bold:
I do arrest your words. Be that you are,
That is a woman; if you be more, you're none.   10
If you be one (as you are well express'd
By all external warrants) show it now,
By putting on the destin'd livery.
ISABELLA: I have no tongue but one; gentle my Lord,
Let me entreat you speak the former language.   15
ANGELO: Plainly conceive I love you.
ISABELLA: My brother did love Juliet,
And you tell me that he shall die for 't.
ANGELO: He shall not Isabel if you give me love.
ISABELLA: I know your virtue hath a license in 't,   20
Which seems a little fouler than it is,
To pluck on others.
ANGELO: Believe me on mine honour,
My words express my purpose.
ISABELLA: Ha? Little honour, to be much believ'd,   25
And most pernicious purpose: Seeming, seeming.
I will proclaim thee Angelo, look for 't.
Sign me a present pardon for my brother,
Or with an outstretch'd throat I'll tell the world aloud
What man thou art.   30
ANGELO: Who will believe thee Isabel?
My unsoil'd name, th' austereness of my life,
My vouch against you, and my place i' th' State,

Will so your accusation overweigh,
That you shall stifle in your own report,
And smell of calumny. I have begun,
And now I give my sensual race, the rein,
5   Fit thy consent to my sharp appetite,
Lay by all nicety, and prolixious blushes
That banish what they sue for: Redeem thy brother,
By yielding up thy body to my will,
Or else he must not only die the death,
10 But thy unkindness shall his death draw out
To lingering sufferance: Answer me tomorrow,
Or by the affection that now guides me most,
I'll prove a tyrant to him. As for you,
Say what you can; my false, o'erweighs your true.
15   *Exit*.
   ISABELLA: To whom should I complain? Did I tell this,
Who would believe me? O perilous mouths
That bear in them, one and the selfsame tongue,
Either of condemnation, or approof,
20 Bidding the Law make curtsy to their will,
Hooking both right and wrong to th' appetite,
To follow as it draws. I'll to my brother,
Though he hath fall'n by prompture of the blood,
Yet hath he in him such a mind of honour,
25 That had he twenty heads to tender down
On twenty bloody blocks, he'd yield them up,
Before his sister should her body stoop
To such abhorr'd pollution.
Then Isabel live chaste, and brother, die;
30 More than our brother, is our chastity.
I'll tell him yet of Angelo's request,
And fit his mind to death, for his soul's rest.
                                    Exit.

Enter Duke (as a friar), Claudio, and Provost.

DUKE: So then you hope of pardon from Lord Angelo?

CLAUDIO: The miserable have no other medicine
    But only hope: I've hope to live, and am prepar'd to die. 5

DUKE: Be absolute for death: either death or life
    Shall thereby be the sweeter. Reason thus with life:
    If I do lose thee, I do lose a thing
    That none but fools would keep: a breath thou art,
    Servile to all the skyey influences, 10
    That dost this habitation where thou keep'st
    Hourly afflict: Merely, thou art death's fool,
    For him thou labour'st by thy flight to shun,
    And yet runn'st toward him still. Thou art not noble,
    For all th' accommodations that thou bear'st 15
    Are nurs'd by baseness: Thou'rt by no means valiant,
    For thou dost fear the soft and tender fork
    Of a poor worm: thy best of rest is sleep,
    And that thou oft provok'st, yet grossly fear'st
    Thy death, which is no more. Thou art not thyself, 20
    For thou exist'st on many a thousand grains
    That issue out of dust. Happy thou art not,
    For what thou hast not, still thou striv'st to get,
    And what thou hast forget'st. Thou are not certain,
    For thy complexion shifts to strange effects, 25
    After the Moon: If thou art rich, thou'rt poor,
    For like an ass, whose back with ingots bows,
    Thou bear'st thy heavy riches but a journey,
    And death unloads thee: Friend hast thou none,
    For thine own bowels which do call thee sire, 30
    The mere effusion of thy proper loins,
    Do curse the gout, serpigo, and the rheum

For ending thee no sooner. Thou hast nor youth, nor
   age
But as it were an after-dinner's sleep
Dreaming on both, for all thy blessed youth
5   Becomes as aged, and doth beg the alms
Of palsied eld: and when thou art old, and rich,
Thou hast neither heat, affection, limb, nor beauty
To make thy riches pleasant: what's yet in this
That bears the name of life? Yet in this life
10 Lie hid moe thousand deaths; yet death we fear
That makes these odds, all even.
CLAUDIO: I humbly thank you.
To sue to live, I find I seek to die,
And, seeking death, find life: Let it come on.
15   *Enter Isabella.*
ISABELLA: What hoa? Peace here; Grace, and good
company.
PROVOST: Who's there? Come in, the wish deserves a
welcome.
20 DUKE: Dear sir, ere long I'll visit you again.
CLAUDIO: Most holy Sir, I thank you.
ISABELLA: My business is a word or two with Claudio.
PROVOST: And very welcome: look Signior, here's your
sister.
25 DUKE: Provost, a word with you.
PROVOST: As many as you please.
DUKE: Bring me to hear them speak, where I may be
conceal'd.
CLAUDIO: Now sister, what's the comfort?
30 ISABELLA: Why,
As all comforts are: most good, most good indeed,
Lord Angelo having affairs to heaven
Intends you for his swift Ambassador,

Where you shall be an everlasting Leiger;
Therefore your best appointment make with speed,
Tomorrow you set on.

CLAUDIO: Is there no remedy?

ISABELLA: None, but such remedy, as to save a head 5
To cleave a heart in twain.

CLAUDIO: But is there any?

ISABELLA: Yes brother, you may live;
There is a devilish mercy in the Judge,
If you'll implore it, that will free your life, 10
But fetter you till death.

CLAUDIO: Perpetual durance?

ISABELLA: Ay just, perpetual durance, a restraint
Through all the world's vastidity you had
To a determin'd scope. 15

CLAUDIO: But in what nature?

ISABELLA: In such a one, as you consenting to't,
Would bark your honour from that trunk you bear,
And leave you naked.

CLAUDIO: Let me know the point. 20

ISABELLA: Oh, I do fear thee Claudio, and I quake,
Lest thou a feverous life shouldst entertain,
And six or seven winters more respect
Than a perpetual honour. Dar'st thou die?
The sense of death is most in apprehension, 25
And the poor beetle that we tread upon
In corporal sufferance, finds a pang as great,
As when a giant dies.

CLAUDIO: Why give you me this shame?
Think you I can a resolution fetch 30
From flowery tenderness? If I must die,
I will encounter darkness as a bride,
And hug it in mine arms.

ISABELLA: There spake my brother: there my father's
     grave
   Did utter forth a voice. Yes, thou must die:
   Thou art too noble, to conserve a life
5 In base appliances. This outward sainted Deputy,
   Whose settled visage, and deliberate word
   Nips youth i' th' head, and follies doth emmew
   As falcon doth the fowl, is yet a devil:
   His filth within being cast, he would appear
10 A pond, as deep as hell.
   CLAUDIO: The prenzie, Angelo?
   ISABELLA: Oh 'tis the cunning livery of hell,
   The damnest body to invest, and cover
   In prenzie guards; dost thou think Claudio,
15 If I would yield him my virginity
   Thou mightst be freed?
   CLAUDIO: Oh heavens, it cannot be.
   ISABELLA: Yes, he would give 't thee; from this rank
     offence
20 So to offend him still. This night's the time
   That I should do what I abhor to name,
   Or else thou diest tomorrow.
   CLAUDIO: Thou shalt not do't.
   ISABELLA: O, were it but my life,
25 I'd throw it down for your deliverance
   As frankly as a pin.
   CLAUDIO: Thanks dear Isabel.
   ISABELLA: Be ready Claudio, for your death tomorrow.
   CLAUDIO: Yes. Has he affections in him,
30 That thus can make him bite the Law by th' nose,
   When he would force it? Sure it is no sin,
   Or of the deadly seven it is the least.
   ISABELLA: Which is the least?

CLAUDIO: If it were damnable, he being so wise,
　Why would he for the momentary trick
　Be perdurably fin'd? Oh Isabel.
ISABELLA: What says my brother?
CLAUDIO: Death is a fearful thing.　　　　　　　　5
ISABELLA: And shamed life, a hateful.
CLAUDIO: Ay, but to die, and go we know not where,
　To lie in cold obstruction, and to rot,
　This sensible warm motion, to become
　A kneaded clod; And the delighted spirit　　　10
　To bathe in fiery floods, or to reside
　In thrilling region of thick-ribbed ice,
　To be imprison'd in the viewless winds
　And blown with restless violence round about
　The pendent world: or to be worse than worst　15
　Of those, that lawless and incertain thought,
　Imagine howling, 'tis too horrible.
　The weariest, and most loathed worldly life
　That age, ache, penury, and imprisonment
　Can lay on nature, is a paradise　　　　　　　20
　To what we fear of death.
ISABELLA: Alas, alas.
CLAUDIO: Sweet Sister, let me live.
　What sin you do, to save a brother's life,
　Nature dispenses with the deed so far,　　　　25
　That it becomes a virtue.
ISABELLA: O you beast,
　O faithless coward, oh dishonest wretch,
　Wilt thou be made a man, out of my vice?
　Is't not a kind of incest, to take life　　　　　30
　From thine own sister's shame? What should I think,
　Heaven shield my Mother play'd my Father fair:
　For such a warped slip of wilderness

Ne'er issu'd from his blood. Take my defiance,
Die, perish: Might but my bending down
Reprieve thee from thy fate, it should proceed.
I'll pray a thousand prayers for thy death,
5   No word to save thee.

CLAUDIO: Nay hear me Isabel.

ISABELLA: Oh fie, fie, fie:
Thy sin's not accidental, but a trade;
Mercy to thee would prove itself a bawd,
10   'Tis best that thou diest quickly.

CLAUDIO: Oh hear me Isabella.

DUKE: Vouchsafe a word, young sister, but one word.

ISABELLA: What is your will?

DUKE: Might you dispense with your leisure, I would by
15   and by have some speech with you: the satisfaction I
would require, is likewise your own benefit.

ISABELLA: I have no superfluous leisure, my stay must be
stolen out of other affairs: but I will attend you awhile.

DUKE: Son, I have overheard what hath pass'd between
20   you and your sister. Angelo had never the purpose to
corrupt her; only he hath made an assay of her virtue,
to practise his judgement with the disposition of natures.
She (having the truth of honour in her) hath made him
that gracious denial, which he is most glad to receive: I
25   am confessor to Angelo, and I know this to be true,
therefore prepare yourself to death: do not satisfy your
resolution with hopes that are fallible, tomorrow you
must die, go to your knees, and make ready.

CLAUDIO: Let me ask my sister pardon. I am so out of
30   love with life, that I will sue to be rid of it.

DUKE: Hold you there: farewell:

               Exit Claudio.

Provost, a word with you.

PROVOST: What's your will (father)?

DUKE: That now you are come, you will be gone: Leave me awhile with the maid, my mind promises with my habit, no loss shall touch her by my company.

PROVOST: In good time.   5

Exit.

DUKE: The hand that hath made you fair, hath made you good: the goodness that is cheap in beauty, makes beauty brief in goodness; but grace being the soul of your complexion, shall keep the body of it ever fair: 10 the assault that Angelo hath made to you, Fortune hath convey'd to my understanding; and but that frailty hath examples for his falling, I should wonder at Angelo. How will you do to content this Substitute, and to save your Brother?   15

ISABELLA: I am now going to resolve him: I had rather my brother die by the Law, than my son should be unlawfully born. But (oh) how much is the good Duke deceiv'd in Angelo: if ever he return, and I can speak to him, I will open my lips in vain, or discover his govern- 20 ment.

DUKE: That shall not be much amiss; yet, as the matter now stands, he will avoid your accusation: he made trial of you only. Therefore fasten your ear on my advisings, to the love I have in doing good; a remedy pre- 25 sents itself. I do make myself believe that you may most uprighteously do a poor wronged Lady a merited benefit; redeem your brother from the angry Law; do no stain to your own gracious person, and much please the absent Duke, if peradventure he shall ever return to have hear- 30 ing of this business.

ISABELLA: Let me hear you speak farther; I have spirit to do anything that appears not foul in the truth of my spirit.

DUKE: Virtue is bold, and goodness never fearful: Have you not heard speak of Mariana the sister of Frederick the great soldier, who miscarried at sea?

ISABELLA: I have heard of the Lady, and good words went
5 with her name.

DUKE: She should this Angelo have married: was affianced to her oath, and the nuptial appointed: between which time of the contract, and limit of the solemnity, her brother Frederick was wrack'd at sea, having in that
10 perished vessel the dowry of his sister: but mark how heavily this befell to the poor Gentlewoman, there she lost a noble and renowned brother, in his love toward her, ever most kind and natural: with him the portion and sinew of her fortune, her marriage dowry; with
15 both, her combinate husband, this well-seeming Angelo.

ISABELLA: Can this be so? did Angelo so leave her?

DUKE: Left her in her tears, and dried not one of them with his comfort: swallowed his vows whole, pretending in her, discoveries of dishonour: in few, bestow'd her on
20 her own lamentation, which she yet wears for his sake: and he, a marble to her tears, is washed with them, but relents not.

ISABELLA: What a merit were it in death to take this poor maid from the world? what corruption in this life, that
25 it will let this man live? But how out of this can she avail?

DUKE: It is a rupture that you may easily heal: and the cure of it not only saves your brother, but keeps you from dishonour in doing it.

ISABELLA: Show me how (good Father).

30 DUKE: This fore-named maid hath yet in her the continuance of her first affection: his unjust unkindness (that in all reason should have quenched her love) hath (like an impediment in the current) made it more violent and

unruly: Go you to Angelo, answer his requiring with a plausible obedience, agree with his demands to the point: only refer yourself to this advantage; first, that your stay with him may not be long: that the time may have all shadow, and silence in it: and the place answer to con- 5 venience: this being granted in course, and now follows all: we shall advise this wronged maid to stead up your appointment, go in your place: if the encounter acknowledge itself hereafter, it may compel him to her recompence; and here, by this is your brother saved, your 10 honour untainted, the poor Mariana advantaged, and the corrupt Deputy scaled. The maid will I frame, and make fit for his attempt: if you think well to carry this as you may, the doubleness of the benefit defends the deceit from reproof. What think you of it? 15

ISABELLA: The image of it gives me content already, and I trust it will grow to a most prosperous perfection.

DUKE: It lies much in your holding up: haste you speedily to Angelo, if for this night he entreat you to his bed, give him promise of satisfaction: I will presently to S. 20 Luke's, there at the moated grange resides this dejected Mariana; at that place call upon me, and dispatch with Angelo, that it may be quickly.

ISABELLA: I thank you for this comfort: fare you well good father. 25

Exit.

Enter Elbow, Clown, Officers.

ELBOW: Nay, if there be no remedy for it, but that you will needs buy and sell men and women like beasts, we shall have all the world drink brown and white 30 bastard.

DUKE: Oh heavens, what stuff is here.

CLOWN: 'Twas never merry world since of two usuries

the merriest was put down, and the worser allow'd by
order of Law; a furr'd gown to keep him warm; and
furr'd with fox and lambskins too, to signify, that craft
being richer than innocency, stands for the facing.

5 ELBOW: Come your way sir: 'bless you good Father Friar.

DUKE: And you good Brother Father; what offence hath
this man made you, Sir?

ELBOW: Marry Sir, he hath offended the Law; and, Sir,
we take him to be a thief too Sir; for we have found

10 upon him Sir, a strange pick-lock, which we have sent
to the Deputy.

DUKE: Fie, sirrah, a bawd, a wicked bawd,
The evil that thou causest to be done,
That is thy means to live. Do thou but think

15 What 'tis to cram a maw, or clothe a back
From such a filthy vice: say to thyself,
From their abominable and beastly touches
I drink, I eat, array myself, and live:
Canst thou believe thy living is a life,

20 So stinkingly depending? Go mend, go mend.

CLOWN: Indeed, it does stink in some sort, Sir:
But yet Sir I would prove.

DUKE: Nay, if the devil have given thee proofs for sin
Thou wilt prove his. Take him to prison Officer:

25 Correction, and instruction must both work
Ere this rude beast will profit.

ELBOW: He must before the Deputy Sir, he has given him
warning: the Deputy cannot abide a whore-master: if
he be a whore-monger, and comes before him, he were

30 as good go a mile on his errand.

DUKE: That we were all, as some would seem to be
From our faults, as faults from seeming free.

              Enter Lucio.

ELBOW: His neck will come to your waist, a cord sir.

CLOWN: I spy comfort, I cry bail: here's a Gentleman, and a friend of mine.

LUCIO: How now noble Pompey? What, at the wheels of Caesar? Art thou led in triumph? What is there none of Pygmalion's images newly made woman to be had now, for putting the hand in the pocket, and extracting clutch'd? What reply? Ha? What say'st thou to this tune, matter, and method? Is't not drown'd i' th' last rain? Ha? What sayest thou Trot? Is the world as it was man? Which is the way? Is it sad, and few words? Or how? The trick of it?

DUKE: Still thus, and thus: still worse?

LUCIO: How doth my dear morsel, thy mistress? Procures she still, ha?

CLOWN: Troth sir, she hath eaten up all her beef, and she is herself in the tub.

LUCIO: Why 'tis good: It is the right of it: it must be so. Ever your fresh whore, and your powder'd bawd, an unshunn'd consequence, it must be so. Art going to prison Pompey?

CLOWN: Yes faith sir.

LUCIO: Why 'tis not amiss Pompey: farewell: go say I sent thee thither: for debt Pompey? Or how?

ELBOW: For being a bawd, for being a bawd.

LUCIO: Well, then imprison him: if imprisonment be the due of a bawd, why 'tis his right. Bawd is he doubtless, and of antiquity too; Bawd born. Farewell good Pompey: Commend me to the prison Pompey, you will turn good husband now Pompey, you will keep the house.

CLOWN: I hope Sir, your good Worship will be my bail?

LUCIO: No indeed will I not Pompey, it is not the wear: I will pray (Pompey) to increase your bondage. If you

take it not patiently: why, your mettle is the more:
Adieu trusty Pompey.

Bless you Friar.

DUKE: And you.

5 LUCIO: Does Bridget paint still, Pompey? Ha?

ELBOW: Come your ways sir, come.

CLOWN: You will not bail me then Sir?

LUCIO: Then Pompey, nor now, what news abroad
Friar? What news?

10 ELBOW: Come your ways sir, come.

LUCIO: Go to kennel (Pompey) go:

> *Exeunt Elbow, Clown, and Officers.*

What news Friar of the Duke?

DUKE: I know none: can you tell me of any?

15 LUCIO: Some say he is with the Emperor of Russia; other
some, he is in Rome: but where is he think you?

DUKE: I know not where: but wheresoever, I wish him
well.

LUCIO: It was a mad fantastical trick of him to steal from
20   the State, and usurp the beggary he was never born to:
Lord Angelo dukes it well in his absence: he puts trans-
gression to't.

DUKE: He does well in't.

LUCIO: A little more lenity to lechery would do no harm
25   in him: Something too crabbed that way, Friar.

DUKE: It is too general a vice, and severity must cure it.

LUCIO: Yes in good sooth, the vice is of a great kindred; it
is well allied, but it is impossible to extirp it quite, Friar,
till eating and drinking be put down. They say this
30   Angelo was not made by man and woman, after this
downright way of creation: is it true, think you?

DUKE: How should he be made then?

LUCIO: Some report, a sea maid spawn'd him. Some,

that he was begot between two stock-fishes. But it is certain, that when he makes water, his urine is congeal'd ice, that I know to be true: and he is a motion generative, that's infallible.

DUKE: You are pleasant sir, and speak apace. 5

LUCIO: Why, what a ruthless thing is this in him, for the rebellion of a codpiece, to take away the life of a man? Would the Duke that is absent have done this? Ere he would have hang'd a man for the getting a hundred bastards, he would have paid for the nursing a thousand. 10 He had some feeling of the sport, he knew the service, and that instructed him to mercy.

DUKE: I never heard the absent Duke much detected for women, he was not inclin'd that way.

LUCIO: Oh Sir, you are deceiv'd. 15

DUKE: 'Tis not possible.

LUCIO: Who, not the Duke? Yes, your beggar of fifty: and his use was to put a ducat in her clack-dish; the Duke had crotchets in him. He would be drunk too, that let me inform you. 20

DUKE: You do him wrong, surely.

LUCIO: Sir, I was an inward of his: a shy fellow was the Duke, and I believe I know the cause of his withdrawing.

DUKE: What (I prithee) might be the cause?

LUCIO: No, pardon: 'Tis a secret must be lock'd within the 25 teeth and the lips, but this I can let you understand, the greater file of the subject held the Duke to be wise.

DUKE: Wise? Why no question but he was.

LUCIO: A very superficial, ignorant, unweighing fellow.

DUKE: Either this is envy in you, folly, or mistaking: the 30 very stream of his life, and the business he hath helmed, must upon a warranted need, give him a better proclamation. Let him be but testimonied in his own bringings forth, and he shall appear to the envious a scholar, a statesman, and a soldier: therefore you speak unskilfully: or, if your knowledge be more, it is much darken'd in your malice.

5 LUCIO: Sir, I know him, and I love him.

DUKE: Love talks with better knowledge, and knowledge with dearer love.

LUCIO: Come Sir, I know what I know.

DUKE: I can hardly believe that, since you know not what
10 you speak. But if ever the Duke return (as our prayers are he may) let me desire you to make your answer before him: if it be honest you have spoke, you have courage to maintain it; I am bound to call upon you, and, I pray you your name?

15 LUCIO: Sir my name is Lucio, well known to the Duke.

DUKE: He shall know you better Sir, if I may live to report you.

LUCIO: I fear you not.

DUKE: O, you hope the Duke will return no more: or you
20 imagine me too unhurtful an opposite: but indeed I can do you little harm: You'll forswear this again.

LUCIO: I'll be hang'd first: thou art deceiv'd in me Friar. But no more of this: Canst thou tell if Claudio die to-morrow, or no?

25 DUKE: Why should he die Sir?

LUCIO: Why? For filling a bottle with a tundish: I would the Duke we talk of were return'd again: this ungenitur'd Agent will unpeople the Province with continency. Sparrows must not build in his house-eaves, because they
30 are lecherous: The Duke yet would have dark deeds darkly answered, he would never bring them to light: would he were return'd. Marry this Claudio is condemned for untrussing. Farewell good Friar. I prithee

pray for me. The Duke (I say to thee again) would eat
mutton on Fridays. He's now past it, yet (and I say to
thee) he would mouth with a beggar, though she smelt
brown bread and garlic: say that I said so: Farewell.

Exit. 5

DUKE: No might, nor greatness in mortality
Can censure 'scape; back-wounding calumny
The whitest virtue strikes. What King so strong,
Can tie the gall up in the slanderous tongue?
But who comes here? 10

Enter Escalus, Provost, and Bawd.

ESCALUS: Go, away with her to prison.

BAWD: Good my Lord be good to me, your Honour is
accounted a merciful man: good my Lord.

ESCALUS: Double, and treble admonition, and still forfeit 15
in the same kind? This would make mercy swear and
play the Tyrant.

PROVOST: A bawd of eleven years' continuance, may it
please your Honour.

BAWD: My Lord, this is one Lucio's information against 20
me, Mistress Kate Keepdown was with child by him in
the Duke's time, he promis'd her marriage: his child is a
year and a quarter old come Philip and Jacob: I have kept
it myself; and see how he goes about to abuse me.

ESCALUS: That fellow is a fellow of much license: Let him 25
be call'd before us. Away with her to prison: Go to, no
more words. Provost, my brother Angelo will not be
alter'd, Claudio must die tomorrow: Let him be furnish'd
with divines, and have all charitable preparation. If my
brother wrought by my pity, it should not be so with 30
him.

PROVOST: So please you, this Friar hath been with him,
and advis'd him for the entertainment of death.

ESCALUS: Good even, good Father.

DUKE: Bliss, and goodness on you.

ESCALUS: Of whence are you?

DUKE: Not of this Country, though my chance is now
5 To use it for my time: I am a brother
Of gracious Order, come late from the Sea,
In special business from his Holiness.

ESCALUS: What news abroad i' th' World?

DUKE: None, but that there is so great a fever on goodness,
10 that the dissolution of it must cure it. Novelty is only in
request, and it is as dangerous to be aged in any kind of
course, as it is virtuous to be constant in any under-
taking. There is scarce truth enough alive to make
societies secure, but security enough to make fellow-
15 ships accurst: Much upon this riddle runs the wisdom of
the world: This news is old enough, yet it is every day's
news. I pray you Sir, of what disposition was the Duke?

ESCALUS: One, that above all other strifes,
Contended especially to know himself.

20 DUKE: What pleasure was he given to?

ESCALUS: Rather rejoicing to see another merry, than
merry at anything which profess'd to make him rejoice.
A Gentleman of all temperance. But leave we him to his
events, with a prayer they may prove prosperous, and
25 let me desire to know, how you find Claudio prepar'd?
I am made to understand, that you have lent him visitation.

DUKE: He professes to have received no sinister measure
from his Judge, but most willingly humbles himself to
the determination of Justice: yet had he framed to him-
30 self (by the instruction of his frailty) many deceiving
promises of life, which I (by my good leisure) have dis-
credited to him, and now is he resolv'd to die.

ESCALUS: You have paid the heavens your function, and the

prisoner the very debt of your calling. I have labour'd
for the poor Gentleman, to the extremest shore of my
modesty, but my brother Justice have I found so severe,
that he hath forc'd me to tell him, he is indeed Justice.

DUKE: If his own life, answer the straitness of his proceed-   5
ing, it shall become him well: wherein if he chance to
fail he hath sentenc'd himself.

ESCALUS: I am going to visit the prisoner: Fare you well.

DUKE: Peace be with you.

Exeunt Escalus and Provost.   10

He who the sword of Heaven will bear,
Should be as holy, as severe:
Pattern in himself to know,
Grace to stand, and virtue go:
More, nor less to others paying,   15
Than by self-offences weighing.
Shame to him, whose cruel striking,
Kills for faults of his own liking:
Twice treble shame on Angelo,
To weed my vice, and let his grow.   20
Oh, what may man within him hide,
Though Angel on the outward side?
How may likeness made in crimes,
Making practice on the times,
To draw with idle spiders' strings   25
Most ponderous and substantial things?
Craft against vice, I must apply.
With Angelo tonight shall lie
His old betrothed (but despised):
So disguise shall by th' disguised,   30
Pay with falsehood, false exacting,
And perform an old contracting.

Exit.

IV.1

Enter Mariana, and Boy Singing.
Song.

Take, oh, take those lips away,
5   *That so sweetly were forsworn,*
And those eyes; the break of day
   Lights that do mislead the morn;
But my kisses bring again, bring again,
Seals of love, but seal'd in vain, seal'd in vain.

10   *Enter Duke (as a Friar).*

MARIANA: Break off thy song, and haste thee quick away,
Here comes a man of comfort, whose advice
Hath often still'd my brawling discontent.

          Exit Boy.

15 I cry you mercy, Sir, and well could wish
You had not found me here so musical.
Let me excuse me, and believe me so,
My mirth it much displeas'd, but pleas'd my woe.

DUKE: 'Tis good; though Music oft hath such a charm
20 To make bad, good; and good provoke to harm.
I pray you tell me, hath anybody inquir'd for me here
today; much upon this time have I promis'd here to
meet.

MARIANA: You have not been inquir'd after: I have sat
25 here all day.

          Enter Isabell.

DUKE: I do constantly believe you: the time is come even
now. I shall crave your forbearance a little, maybe I will
call upon you anon for some advantage to yourself.

30 MARIANA: I am always bound to you.

          Exit.

DUKE: Very well met, and well come:

What is the news from this good Deputy?

ISABELLA: He hath a garden circummur'd with brick,
    Whose western side is with a vineyard back'd,
    And to that vineyard is a planched gate,
    That makes his opening with this bigger key: 5
    This other doth command a little door,
    Which from the vineyard to the garden leads.
    There have I made my promise upon the
    Heavy middle of the night, to call upon him.

DUKE: But shall you on your knowledge find this way?   10

ISABELLA: I have ta'en a due, and wary note upon 't,
    With whispering, and most guilty diligence,
    In action all of precept, he did show me
    The way twice o'er.

DUKE: Are there no other tokens   15
    Between you 'greed concerning her observance?

ISABELLA: No: none but only a repair i' th' dark,
    And that I have possess'd him, my most stay
    Can be but brief: for I have made him know,
    I have a servant comes with me along   20
    That stays upon me; whose persuasion is,
    I come about my brother.

DUKE: 'Tis well borne up.
    I have not yet made known to Mariana

              Enter Mariana.   25

    A word of this: what hoa, within, come forth,
    I pray you be acquainted with this Maid,
    She comes to do you good.

ISABELLA: I do desire the like.

DUKE: Do you persuade yourself that I respect you?   30

MARIANA: Good Friar, I know you do, and have found it.

DUKE: Take then this your companion by the hand,
    Who hath a story ready for your ear:

    I shall attend your leisure, but make haste,
    The vaporous night approaches.
MARIANA: Will't please you walk aside?
               Exeunt Mariana and Isabella.
5 DUKE: Oh place, and greatness: millions of false eyes
    Are stuck upon thee: volumes of report
    Run with these false, and most contrarious quests
    Upon thy doings: thousand escapes of wit
    Make thee the father of their idle dream,
10 And rack thee in their fancies.
    Welcome, how agreed?
               Enter Mariana and Isabella.
ISABELLA: She'll take the enterprise upon her father,
    If you advise it.
15 DUKE: It is not my consent,
    But my entreaty too.
ISABELLA: Little have you to say
    When you depart from him, but soft and low,
    Remember now my brother.
20 MARIANA: Fear me not.
DUKE: Nor gentle daughter, fear you not at all:
    He is your husband on a pre-contract:
    To bring you thus together 'tis no sin,
    Sith that the justice of your title to him
25 Doth flourish the deceit. Come, let us go,
    Our corn's to reap, for yet our tithe's to sow.
               Exeunt.

IV.2

Enter Provost and Clown.

30 PROVOST: Come hither sirrah; can you cut off a man's head?

CLOWN: If the man be a bachelor Sir, I can: But if he be a married man, he's his wife's head, and I can never cut off a woman's head.

PROVOST: Come sir, leave me your snatches, and yield me a direct answer. Tomorrow morning are to die Claudio and Barnardine: here is in our prison a common executioner, who in his office lacks a helper; if you will take it on you to assist him, it shall redeem you from your gyves: if not, you shall have your full time of imprisonment, and your deliverance with an unpitied whipping; for you have been a notorious bawd.

CLOWN: Sir, I have been an unlawful bawd, time out of mind, but yet I will be content to be a lawful hangman: I would be glad to receive some instruction from my fellow partner.

PROVOST: What hoa, Abhorson: where's Abhorson, there?

Enter Abhorson.

ABHORSON: Do you call sir?

PROVOST: Sirrah, here's a fellow will help you tomorrow in your execution: if you think it meet, compound with him by the year, and let him abide here with you, if not, use him for the present, and dismiss him, he cannot plead his estimation with you: he hath been a bawd.

ABHORSON: A bawd Sir? fie upon him, he will discredit our mystery.

PROVOST: Go to Sir, you weigh equally: a feather will turn the scale.

Exit.

CLOWN: Pray sir, by your good favour: for surely sir, a good favour you have, but that you have a hanging look: Do you call sir, your occupation a Mystery?

ABHORSON: Ay Sir, a Mystery.

CLOWN: Painting Sir, I have heard say, is a Mystery; and
your whores sir, being members of my occupation, using
painting, do prove my occupation, a Mystery: but what
Mystery there should be in hanging, if I should be hang'd,
5   I cannot imagine.

ABHORSON: Sir, it is a Mystery.

CLOWN: Proof.

ABHORSON: Every true man's apparel fits your thief.

CLOWN: If it be too little for your thief, your true man
10   thinks it big enough. If it be too big for your thief, your
thief thinks it little enough: So every true man's apparel
fits your thief.

Enter Provost.

PROVOST: Are you agreed?

15   CLOWN: Sir, I will serve him: for I do find your hangman
is a more penitent trade than your bawd: he doth
oftner ask forgiveness.

PROVOST: You sirrah, provide your block and your axe
tomorrow, four a clock.

20   ABHORSON: Come on (bawd) I will instruct thee in my
trade: follow.

CLOWN: I do desire to learn sir: and I hope, if you have
occasion to use me for your own turn, you shall find me
yare. For truly sir, for your kindness, I owe you a good
25   turn.

Exeunt Clown and Abhorson.

PROVOST: Call hither Barnardine and Claudio:
Th' one has my pity; not a jot the other,
Being a murtherer, though he were my brother.

30   *Enter Claudio.*

Look, here's the warrant Claudio, for thy death,
'Tis now dead midnight, and by eight tomorrow
Thou must be made immortal. Where's Barnardine?

CLAUDIO: As fast lock'd up in sleep as guiltless labour,
  When it lies starkly in the traveller's bones,
  He will not wake.
PROVOST: Who can do good on him?
  Well, go, prepare yourself. But hark, what noise?   5
  Heaven give your spirits comfort: by, and by,
              Exit Claudio.
  I hope it is some pardon, or reprieve
  For the most gentle Claudio. Welcome, Father.
              Enter Duke, as Friar.   10
DUKE: The best, and wholesomest spirits of the night,
  Envelop you, good Provost: who call'd here of late?
PROVOST: None since the curfew rung.
DUKE: Not Isabel?
PROVOST: No.   15
DUKE: They will then ere't be long.
PROVOST: What comfort is for Claudio?
DUKE: There's some in hope.
PROVOST: It is a bitter Deputy.
DUKE: Not so, not so: his life is parallel'd   20
  Even with the stroke and line of his great justice:
  He doth with holy abstinence subdue
  That in himself, which he spurs on his power
  To qualify in others: were he meal'd with that
  Which he corrects, then were he tyrannous,   25
  But this being so, he's just. Now are they come.
              Exit Provost.
  This is a gentle Provost, seldom when
  The steeled jailer is the friend of men:
  How now? what noise? That spirit's possess'd with   30
    haste,
  That wounds th' unsisting postern with these strokes.
              Enter Provost.

PROVOST: There he must stay until the officer
    Arise to let him in: he is call'd up.
DUKE: Have you no countermand for Claudio yet?
    But he must die tomorrow?
5 PROVOST: None Sir, none.
DUKE: As near the dawning Provost, as it is,
    You shall hear more ere morning.
PROVOST: Happily
    You something know: yet I believe there comes
10   No countermand: no such example have we:
    Besides, upon the very siege of Justice,
    Lord Angelo hath to the public ear
    Profess'd the contrary.

               Enter a Messenger.

15 DUKE: This is his Lord's man.
PROVOST: And here comes Claudio's pardon.
MESSENGER: My Lord hath sent you this note,
    And by me this further charge;
    That you swerve not from the smallest article of it,
20   Neither in time, matter, or other circumstance.
    Good morrow: for as I take it, it is almost day.
PROVOST: I shall obey him.

               Exit Messenger.

DUKE: This is his pardon, purchas'd by such sin
25   For which the pardoner himself is in:
    Hence hath offence his quick celerity,
    When it is borne in high authority.
    When Vice makes Mercy; Mercy's so extended,
    That for the fault's love, is th' offender friended.
30   Now Sir, what news?
PROVOST: I told you:
    Lord Angelo (belike) thinking me remiss
    In mine office, awakens me

With this unwonted putting-on, methinks strangely:
For he hath not us'd it before.

DUKE: Pray you let's hear.

The Letter.

Whatsoever you may hear to the contrary, let Claudio be 5
executed by four of the clock, and in the afternoon Barnardine:
For my better satisfaction, let me have Claudio's head sent me
by five. Let this be duly performed with a thought that more
depends on it, than we must yet deliver. Thus fail not to do
your office, as you will answer it at your peril. 10
What say you to this Sir?

DUKE: What is that Barnardine, who is to be executed in
th' afternoon?

PROVOST: A Bohemian born: but here nurs'd up and
bred, one that is a prisoner nine years old. 15

DUKE: How came it, that the absent Duke had not either
deliver'd him to his liberty, or executed him? I have
heard it was ever his manner to do so.

PROVOST: His friends still wrought reprieves for him:
And indeed his fact till now in the government of Lord 20
Angelo, came not to an undoubtful proof.

DUKE: It is now apparent?

PROVOST: Most manifest, and not denied by himself.

DUKE: Hath he borne himself penitently in prison? How
seems he to be touch'd? 25

PROVOST: A man that apprehends death no more dread-
fully, but as a drunken sleep, careless, wreakless, and fear-
less of what's past, present, or to come: insensible of
mortality, and desperately mortal.

DUKE: He wants advice. 30

PROVOST: He will hear none: he hath evermore had the
liberty of the prison: give him leave to escape hence, he
would not. Drunk many times a day, if not many days

entirely drunk. We have very oft awak'd him as if to
carry him to execution, and show'd him a seeming
warrant for it, it hath not moved him at all.

DUKE: More of him anon: There is written in your brow
5   Provost, honesty and constancy; if I read it not truly,
my ancient skill beguiles me: but in the boldness of my
cunning, I will lay myself in hazard: Claudio, whom
here you have warrant to execute, is no greater forfeit to
the Law, than Angelo who hath sentenc'd him. To make
10   you understand this in a manifested effect, I crave but
four days' respite: for the which, you are to do me both a
present, and a dangerous courtesy.

PROVOST: Pray Sir, in what?

DUKE: In the delaying death.

15 PROVOST: Alack, how may I do it? Having the hour
limited, and an express command, under penalty, to deliver his head in the view of Angelo? I may make my
case as Claudio's, to cross this in the smallest.

DUKE: By the vow of mine Order, I warrant you,
20   If my instructions may be your guide,
Let this Barnardine be this morning executed,
And his head borne to Angelo.

PROVOST: Angelo hath seen them both,
And will discover the favour.

25 DUKE: Oh, death's a great disguiser, and you may add to
it; Shave the head, and tie the beard, and say it was the
desire of the penitent to be so bar'd before his death:
You know the course is common. If anything fall to you
upon this, more than thanks and good fortune, by the
30   Saint whom I profess, I will plead against it with my life.

PROVOST: Pardon me, good Father, it is against my oath.

DUKE: Were you sworn to the Duke, or to the Deputy?

PROVOST: To him, and to his Substitutes.

DUKE: You will think you have made no offence, if the
Duke avouch the justice of your dealing?

PROVOST: But what likelihood is in that?

DUKE: Not a resemblance, but a certainty; yet since I see
you fearful, that neither my coat, integrity, nor per- 5
suasion, can with ease attempt you, I will go further than
I meant, to pluck all fears out of you. Look you Sir, here
is the hand and seal of the Duke: you know the character
I doubt not, and the signet is not strange to you?

PROVOST: I know them both. 10

DUKE: The contents of this, is the return of the Duke; you
shall anon over-read it at your pleasure: where you shall
find within these two days, he will be here. This is a thing
that Angelo knows not, for he this very day receives
letters of strange tenor, perchance of the Duke's death, 15
perchance entering into some Monastery, but by
chance nothing of what is writ. Look, th' unfolding Star
calls up the shepherd; put not yourself into amazement,
how these things should be; all difficulties are but easy
when they are known. Call your executioner, and off 20
with Barnardine's head: I will give him a present shrift,
and advise him for a better place. Yet you are amaz'd,
but this shall absolutely resolve you: Come away, it is
almost clear dawn.

Exeunt. 25

IV. 3

Enter Clown.

CLOWN: I am as well acquainted here, as I was in our
house of profession: one would think it were Mistress
Overdone's own house, for here be many of her old cus- 30
tomers. First, here's young Master Rash, he's in for a

commodity of brown paper, and old ginger, nine score and seventeen pounds, of which he made five marks ready money: marry then, ginger was not much in request, for the old women were all dead. Then is there
5 here one Master Caper, at the suit of Master Threepile the Mercer, for some four suits of peach-coloured satin, which now peaches him a beggar. Then have we here, young Dizy, and young Master Deep-vow, and Master Copperspur, and Master Starve-lackey the rapier and
10 dagger man, and young Drop-heir that kill'd lusty Pudding, and Master Forthlight the tilter, and brave Master Shooty the great traveller, and wild Half-can that stabb'd Pots, and I think forty more, all great doers in our trade, and are now for the Lord's sake.

15   *Enter Abhorson.*

ABHORSON: Sirrah, bring Barnardine hither.

CLOWN: Master Barnardine, you must rise and be hang'd, Master Barnardine.

ABHORSON: What hoa, Barnardine.

20   *Barnardine within.*

BARNARDINE: A pox o' your throats: who makes that noise there? What are you?

CLOWN: Your friends Sir, the hangman: You must be so good Sir, to rise and be put to death.

25 BARNARDINE: Away you rogue, away, I am sleepy.

ABHORSON: Tell him he must awake, and that quickly too.

CLOWN: Pray Master Barnardine, awake till you are executed, and sleep afterward.

ABHORSON: Go in to him, and fetch him out.

30 CLOWN: He is coming Sir, he is coming: I hear his straw rustle.

                    Enter Barnardine.

ABHORSON: Is the axe upon the block, sirrah?

CLOWN: Very ready Sir.

BARNARDINE: How now Abhorson?
What's the news with you?

ABHORSON: Truly Sir, I would desire you to clap into
your prayers: for look you, the warrant's come.

BARNARDINE: You rogue, I have been drinking all night,
I am not fitted for 't.

CLOWN: Oh, the better Sir: for he that drinks all night,
and is hanged betimes in the morning, may sleep the
sounder all the next day.

Enter Duke as Friar.

ABHORSON: Look you Sir, here comes your ghostly
Father: do we jest now, think you?

DUKE: Sir, induced by my charity, and hearing how hastily
you are to depart, I am come to advise you, comfort you,
and pray with you.

BARNARDINE: Friar, not I: I have been drinking hard all
night, I will have more time to prepare me, or they shall
beat out my brains with billets: I will not consent to die
this day, that's certain.

DUKE: Oh sir, you must: and therefore I beseech you
Look forward on the journey you shall go.

BARNARDINE: I swear I will not die today for any man's
persuasion.

DUKE: But hear you:

BARNARDINE: Not a word: if you have anything to say
to me, come to my ward; for thence will not I today.

Enter Provost.

DUKE: Unfit to live, or die: Oh gravel heart.
After him (fellows) bring him to the block.

Exeunt Abhorson and Clown.

PROVOST: Now Sir, how do you find the prisoner?

DUKE: A creature unprepar'd, unmeet for death,

And to transport him in the mind he is,
Were damnable.
PROVOST: Here in the prison, Father,
There died this morning of a cruel fever,
5 One Ragozine, a most notorious pirate,
A man of Claudio's years: his beard, and head
Just of his colour. What if we do omit
This reprobate, till he were well inclin'd,
And satisfy the Deputy with the visage
10 . Of Ragozine, more like to Claudio?
DUKE: Oh, 'tis an accident that heaven provides:
Dispatch it presently, the hour draws on
Prefix'd by Angelo: See this be done,
And sent according to command, whiles I
15 Persuade this rude wretch willingly to die.
PROVOST: This shall be done (good Father) presently:
But Barnardine must die this afternoon,
And how shall we continue Claudio,
To save me from the danger that might come,
20 If he were known alive?
DUKE: Let this be done,
Put them in secret holds, both Barnardine and Claudio,
Ere twice the Sun hath made his journal greeting
To the under generation, you shall find
25 Your safety manifested.
PROVOST: I am your free dependant.
                    Exit.
DUKE: Quick, dispatch, and send the head to Angelo.
Now will I write letters to Angelo.
30 (The Provost, he shall bear them) whose contents
Shall witness to him I am near at home:
And that by great injunctions I am bound
To enter publicly: him I'll desire

To meet me at the consecrated Fount,
A league below the City: and from thence,
By cold gradation, and well-balanc'd form,
We shall proceed with Angelo.

Enter Provost.   5

PROVOST: Here is the head, I'll carry it myself.

DUKE: Convenient is it: Make a swift return,
For I would commune with you of such things,
That want no ear but yours.

PROVOST: I'll make all speed.   10

Exit.

Isabell within.

ISABELLA: Peace hoa, be here.

DUKE: The tongue of Isabel. She's come to know,
If yet her brother's pardon be come hither: 15
But I will keep her ignorant of her good,
To make her heavenly comforts of despair,
When it is least expected.

Enter Isabella.

ISABELLA: Hoa, by your leave.   20

DUKE: Good morning to you, fair, and gracious daughter.

ISABELLA: The better given me by so holy a man,
Hath yet the Deputy sent my brother's pardon?

DUKE: He hath releas'd him, Isabel, from the world,
His head is off, and sent to Angelo.   25

ISABELLA: Nay, but it is not so.

DUKE: It is no other,
Show your wisdom daughter in your close patience.

ISABELLA: Oh, I will to him and pluck out his eyes.

DUKE: You shall not be admitted to his sight.   30

ISABELLA: Unhappy Claudio, wretched Isabel,
Injurious world, most damned Angelo.

DUKE: This nor hurts him, nor profits you a jot,
Forbear it therefore, give your cause to heaven.
Mark what I say, which you shall find
By every syllable a faithful verity.
5 . The Duke comes home tomorrow: nay dry your eyes,
One of our covent, and his confessor
Gives me this instance: Already he hath carried
Notice to Escalus and Angelo,
Who do prepare to meet him at the gates,
10 There to give up their power: If you can pace your
wisdom,
In that good path that I would wish it go,
And you shall have your bosom on this wretch,
Grace of the Duke, revenges to your heart,
15 And general honour.
ISABELLA: I am directed by you.
DUKE: This letter then to Friar Peter give,
'Tis that he sent me of the Duke's return:
Say, by this token, I desire his company
20 At Mariana's house tonight. Her cause, and yours
I'll perfect him withal, and he shall bring you
Before the Duke; and to the head of Angelo
Accuse him home and home. For my poor self,
I am combined by a sacred vow,
25 And shall be absent. Wend you with this letter:
Command these fretting waters from your eyes
With a light heart; trust not my holy Order
If I pervert your course: who's here?

Enter Lucio.

30 LUCIO: Good even;
Friar, where's the Provost?
DUKE: Not within Sir.
LUCIO: Oh pretty Isabella, I am pale at mine heart, to see

thine eyes so red: thou must be patient; I am fain to
dine and sup with water and bran: I dare not for my
head fill my belly. One fruitful meal would set me to't:
but they say the Duke will be here tomorrow. By my
troth Isabel I lov'd thy brother, if the old fantastical 5
Duke of dark corners had been at home, he had lived.

Exit Isabella.

DUKE: Sir, the Duke is marvellous little beholding to your
reports, but the best is, he lives not in them.

LUCIO: Friar, thou knowest not the Duke so well as I do: 10
he's a better woodman than thou tak'st him for.

DUKE: Well: you'll answer this one day. Fare ye well.

LUCIO: Nay tarry, I'll go along with'thee,
I can tell thee pretty tales of the Duke.

DUKE: You have told me too many of him already sir if 15
they be true: if not true, none were enough.

LUCIO: I was once before him for getting a wench with
child.

DUKE: Did you such a thing?

LUCIO: Yes marry did I: but I was fain to forswear it, they 20
would else have married me to the rotten medlar.

DUKE: Sir your company is fairer than honest, rest you
well.

LUCIO: By my troth I'll go with thee to the lane's end: if
bawdy talk offend you, we'll have very little of it: nay 25
Friar, I am a kind of burr, I shall stick.

Exeunt.

IV.4

Enter Angelo and Escalus.

ESCALUS: Every letter he hath writ, hath disvouch'd other. 30

ANGELO: In most uneven and distracted manner, his

actions show much like to madness, pray heaven his
wisdom be not tainted: and why meet him at the gates
and redeliver our authorities there?

ESCALUS: I guess not.

5 ANGELO: And why should we proclaim it in an hour before his entring, that if any crave redress of injustice, they
should exhibit their petitions in the street?

ESCALUS: He shows his reason for that: to have a dispatch
of complaints, and to deliver us from devices hereafter,
10 which shall then have no power to stand against us.

ANGELO: Well: I beseech you let it be proclaim'd betimes
i' th' morn. I'll call you at your house: give notice to
such men of sort and suit as are to meet him.

ESCALUS: I shall sir: fare you well.

15   *Exit.*

ANGELO: Good night.
    This deed unshapes me quite, makes me unpregnant
    And dull to all proceedings. A deflower'd maid,
    And by an eminent body, that enforc'd
20   The Law against it? But that her tender shame
    Will not proclaim against her maiden loss,
    How might she tongue me? yet reason dares her no,
    For my authority bears of a credent bulk,
    That no particular scandal once can touch
25   But it confounds the breather. He should have liv'd,
    Save that his riotous youth with dangerous sense
    Might in the times to come have ta'en revenge
    By so receiving a dishonour'd life
    With ransom of such shame: would yet he had lived.
30   Alack, when once our grace we have forgot,
    Nothing goes right, we would, and we would not.
                            Exit.

IV.5

Enter Duke and Friar Peter.

DUKE: These letters at fit time deliver me.
 The Provost knows our purpose and our plot,
 The matter being afoot, keep your instruction   5
 And hold you ever to our special drift,
 Though sometimes you do blench from this to that
 As cause doth minister: Go call at Flavius' house,
 And tell him where I stay: give the like notice
 To Valencius, Rowland, and to Crassus,   10
 And bid them bring the trumpets to the gate:
 But send me Flavius first.
FRIAR PETER: It shall be speeded well.
Exit.
Enter Varrius.   15
DUKE: I thank thee Varrius, thou hast made good haste,
 Come, we will walk: There's other of our friends
 Will greet us here anon: my gentle Varrius.
Exeunt.

IV.6   20

Enter Isabella and Mariana.

ISABELLA: To speak so indirectly I am loath,
 I would say the truth, but to accuse him so,
 That is your part, yet I am advis'd to do it,
 He says, to veil full purpose.   25
MARIANA: Be rul'd by him.
ISABELLA: Besides he tells me, that if peradventure
 He speak against me on the adverse side,
 I should not think it strange, for 'tis a physic
 That's bitter, to sweet end.   30

Enter Peter.

MARIANA: I would Friar Peter—

ISABELLA: Oh peace, the Friar is come.

FRIAR PETER: Come I have found you out a stand most
5   fit,
       Where you may have such vantage on the Duke
       He shall not pass you:
       Twice have the trumpets sounded,
       The generous, and gravest citizens
10   Have hent the gates, and very near upon
       The Duke is entering:
       Therefore hence away.

Exeunt.

V.1

15   *Enter Duke, Varrius, Lords, Angelo, Escalus,*
                 Lucio, Citizens, at several doors.

DUKE: My very worthy cousin, fairly met;
     Our old, and faithful friend, we are glad to see you.

ANGELO AND ESCALUS: Happy return be to your royal
20   grace.

DUKE: Many and hearty thankings to you both:
     We have made inquiry of you, and we hear
     Such goodness of your justice, that our soul
     Cannot but yield you forth to public thanks
25   Forerunning more requital.

ANGELO: You make my bonds still greater.

DUKE: Oh your desert speaks loud, and I should wrong it
     To lock it in the wards of covert bosom
     When it deserves with characters of brass
30   A forted residence 'gainst the tooth of time,
     And razure of oblivion: Give me your hand

And let the subject see, to make them know
That outward courtesies would fain proclaim
Favours that keep within: Come Escalus,
You must walk by us, on your other hand:
And good supporters are you.   5

Enter Peter and Isabella.

FRIAR PETER: Now is your time,
Speak loud, and kneel before him.

ISABELLA: Justice, O royal Duke, vail your regard
Upon a wrong'd (I would fain have said a maid)   10
O worthy Prince, dishonour not your eye
By throwing it on any other object,
Till you have heard me, in my true complaint,
And given me justice, justice, justice, justice.

DUKE: Relate your wrongs;   15
In what, by whom? be brief:
Here is Lord Angelo shall give you justice,
Reveal yourself to him.

ISABELLA: O worthy Duke,
You bid me seek redemption of the devil,   20
Hear me yourself: for that which I must speak
Must either punish me, not being believ'd,
Or wring redress from you:
Hear me: oh hear me, here.

ANGELO: My Lord, her wits I fear me are not firm: 25
She hath been a suitor to me, for her brother
Cut off by course of Justice.

ISABELLA: By course of Justice.

ANGELO: And she will speak most bitterly, and strange.

ISABELLA: Most strange: but yet most truly will I speak, 30
That Angelo's forsworn, is it not strange?
That Angelo's a murtherer, is't not strange?
That Angelo is an adulterous thief,

 A hypocrite, a virgin-violator,
 Is it not strange? and strange?
DUKE: Nay, it is ten times strange.
ISABELLA: It is not truer he is Angelo,
5 Than this is all as true, as it is strange;
 Nay, it is ten times true, for truth is truth
 To th' end of reckoning.
DUKE: Away with her: poor soul
 She speaks this, in th' infirmity of sense.
10 ISABELLA: Oh Prince, I conjure thee, as thou believ'st
 There is another comfort, than this world,
 That thou neglect me not, with that opinion
 That I am touch'd with madness: make not impossible
 That which but seems unlike, 'tis not impossible
15 But one, the wicked'st caitiff on the ground
 May seem as shy, as grave, as just, as absolute
 As Angelo: even so may Angelo
 In all his dressings, characts, titles, forms,
 Be an arch-villain: Believe it, royal Prince
20 If he be less, he's nothing, but he's more,
 Had I more name for badness.
DUKE: By mine honesty
 If she be mad, as I believe no other,
 Her madness hath the oddest frame of sense,
25 Such a dependency of thing, on thing,
 As e'er I heard in madness.
ISABELLA: Oh gracious Duke
 Harp not on that; nor do not banish reason
 For inequality, but let your reason serve
30 To make the truth appear, where it seems hid,
 And hide the false seems true.
DUKE: Many that are not mad
 Have sure more lack of reason:

What would you say?

ISABELLA: I am the sister of one Claudio,
Condemn'd upon the Act of Fornication
To lose his head, condemn'd by Angelo,
I, (in probation of a Sisterhood)   5
Was sent to by my brother; one Lucio
As then the messenger.

LUCIO: That's I, and't like your Grace:
I came to her from Claudio, and desir'd her
To try her gracious fortune with Lord Angelo,   10
For her poor brother's pardon.

ISABELLA: That's he indeed.

DUKE: You were not bid to speak.

LUCIO: No, my good Lord,
Nor wish'd to hold my peace.   15

DUKE: I wish you now then,
Pray you take note of it: and when you have
A business for yourself, pray heaven you then
Be perfect.

LUCIO: I warrant your honour.   20

DUKE: The warrant's for yourself: take heed to't.

ISABELLA: This Gentleman told somewhat of my tale.

LUCIO: Right.

DUKE: It may be right, but you are i' the wrong
To speak before your time: proceed.   25

ISABELLA: I went
To this pernicious caitiff Deputy.

DUKE: That's somewhat madly spoken.

ISABELLA: Pardon it,
The phrase is to the matter.   30

DUKE: Mended again: the matter: proceed.

ISABELLA: In brief, to set the needless process by:
How I persuaded, how I pray'd, and kneel'd,

How he refell'd me, and how I replied
(For this was of much length) the vile conclusion
I now begin with grief, and shame to utter.
He would not, but by gift of my chaste body
5   To his concupiscible intemperate lust,
Release my brother; and after much debatement,
My sisterly remorse, confutes mine honour,
And I did yield to him: But the next morn betimes,
His purpose surfeiting, he sends a warrant
10   For my poor brother's head.
DUKE: This is most likely.
ISABELLA: Oh that it were as like as it is true.
DUKE: By heaven (fond wretch) thou know'st not what
      thou speak'st,
15   Or else thou art suborn'd against his honour
In hateful practice: first his integrity
Stands without blemish: next it imports no reason,
That with such vehemency he should pursue
Faults proper to himself: if he had so offended,
20   He would have weigh'd thy brother by himself,
And not have cut him off: someone hath set you on:
Confess the truth, and say by whose advice
Thou cam'st here to complain.
ISABELLA: And is this all?
25   Then oh you blessed Ministers above
Keep me in patience, and with ripened time
Unfold the evil, which is here wrapp'd up
In countenance: heaven shield your Grace from woe,
As I thus wrong'd, hence unbelieved go.
30   DUKE: I know you'd fain be gone: An officer:
To prison with her: Shall we thus permit
A blasting and a scandalous breath to fall,
On him so near us? This needs must be a practice;

Who knew of your intent and coming hither?
ISABELLA: One that I would were here, Friar Lodowick.
DUKE: A ghostly Father, belike:
Who knows that Lodowick?
LUCIO: My Lord, I know him, 'tis a meddling friar,⠀⠀⠀⠀⠀5
I do not like the man: had he been lay my Lord,
For certain words he spake against your Grace
In your retirement, I had swing'd him soundly.
DUKE: Words against me? this' a good Friar belike
And to set on this wretched woman here⠀⠀⠀⠀⠀10
Against our Substitute: Let this Friar be found.
LUCIO: But yesternight my Lord, she and that Friar,
I saw them at the prison: a saucy Friar,
A very scurvy fellow.
FRIAR PETER: Blessed be your royal Grace:⠀⠀⠀⠀⠀15
I have stood by my Lord, and I have heard
Your royal ear abus'd: first hath this woman
Most wrongfully accus'd your Substitute,
Who is as free from touch, or soil with her
As she from one ungot.⠀⠀⠀⠀⠀20
DUKE: We did believe no less.
Know you that Friar Lodowick that she speaks of?
FRIAR PETER: I know him for a man divine and holy,
Not scurvy, nor a temporary meddler
As he's reported by this Gentleman:⠀⠀⠀⠀⠀25
And on my trust, a man that never yet
Did (as he vouches) mis-report your Grace.
LUCIO: My Lord, most villainously, believe it.
FRIAR PETER: Well: he in time may come to clear him-
self;⠀⠀⠀⠀⠀30
But at this instant he is sick, my Lord:
Of a strange fever: upon his mere request
Being come to knowledge, that there was complaint

Intend'd 'gainst Lord Angelo, came I hither
To speak as from his mouth, what he doth know
Is true, and false: And what he with his oath
And all probation will make up full clear
5   Whensoever he's convented: First for this woman,
To justify this worthy nobleman
So vulgarly, and personally accus'd,
Her shall you hear disproved to her eyes,
Till she herself confess it.
10 DUKE: Good Friar, let's hear it:
Do you not smile at this, Lord Angelo?
Oh heaven, the vanity of wretched fools.
Give us some seats. Come Cousin Angelo,
In this I'll be impartial: be you judge
15   Of your own cause: Is this the witness Friar?
                    Enter Mariana.
First, let her show her face, and after, speak.
MARIANA: Pardon my Lord, I will not show my face
Until my husband bid me.
20 DUKE: What, are you married?
MARIANA: No my Lord.
DUKE: Are you a maid?
MARIANA: No my Lord.
DUKE: A widow then?
25 MARIANA: Neither, my Lord.
DUKE: Why you are nothing then: neither maid, widow,
nor wife?
LUCIO: My Lord, she may be a punk: for many of them
are neither maid, widow, nor wife.
30 DUKE: Silence that fellow: I would he had some cause to
prattle for himself.
LUCIO: Well my Lord.
MARIANA: My Lord, I do confess I ne'er was married,

And I confess besides, I am no maid.
I have known my husband, yet my husband
Knows not, that ever he knew me.

LUCIO: He was drunk then, my Lord, it can be no better.

DUKE: For the benefit of silence, would thou wert so too.   5

LUCIO: Well, my Lord.

DUKE: This is no witness for Lord Angelo.

MARIANA: Now I come to't, my Lord.
She that accuses him of fornication,
In selfsame manner, doth accuse my husband,   10
And charges him, my Lord, with such a time,
When I'll depose I had him in mine arms
With all th' effect of love.

ANGELO: Charges she moe than me?

MARIANA: Not that I know.   15

DUKE: No? you say your husband.

MARIANA: Why just, my Lord, and that is Angelo,
Who thinks he knows, that he ne'er knew my body,
But knows, he thinks, that he knows Isabel's.

ANGELO: This is a strange abuse: Let's see thy face.   20

MARIANA: My husband bids me, now I will unmask.
This is that face, thou cruel Angelo,
Which once thou swor'st, was worth the looking on:
This is the hand, which with a vow'd contract
Was fast belock'd in thine: This is the body   25
That took away the match from Isabel,
And did supply thee at thy garden-house
In her imagin'd person.

DUKE: Know you this woman?

LUCIO: Carnally she says.   30

DUKE: Sirrah, no more.

LUCIO: Enough my Lord.

ANGELO: My Lord, I must confess, I know this woman,

And five years since there was some speech of marriage
Betwixt myself, and her: which was broke off,
Partly for that her promis'd proportions
Came short of composition: But in chief
5   For that her reputation was disvalued
In levity: Since which time of five years
I never spake her with, saw her, nor heard from her
Upon my faith, and honour.

MARIANA: Noble Prince,
10   As there comes light from heaven, and words from
          breath,
As there is sense in truth, and truth in virtue,
I am affianced this man's wife, as strongly
As words could make up vows: And my good Lord,
15   But Tuesday night last gone, in's garden house,
He knew me as a wife. As this is true,
Let me in safety raise me from my knees,
Or else for ever be confixed here
A marble monument.

20 ANGELO: I did but smile till now;
Now, good my Lord, give me the scope of Justice,
My patience here is touch'd: I do perceive
These poor informal women, are no more
But instruments of some more mightier member
25   That sets them on. Let me have way, my Lord
To find this practice out.

DUKE: Ay, with my heart,
And punish them to your height of pleasure.
Thou foolish Friar, and thou pernicious woman
30   Compact with her that's gone: think'st thou, thy oaths,
Though they would swear down each particular Saint,
Were testimonies against his worth, and credit
That's seal'd in approbation? you, Lord Escalus

Sit with my cousin, lend him your kind pains
To find out this abuse, whence 'tis deriv'd.
There is another Friar that set them on,
Let him be sent for.

FRIAR PETER: Would he were here, my Lord, for he in-   5
    deed
Hath set the women on to this complaint;
Your Provost knows the place where he abides,
And he may fetch him.

DUKE: Go, do it instantly.   10

Exit Provost.

And you, my noble and well-warranted cousin
Whom it concerns to hear this matter forth,
Do with your injuries as seems you best
In any chastisement; I for a while   15
Will leave you; but stir not you till you have
Well determin'd upon these slanderers.

Exit.

ESCALUS: My Lord, we'll do it throughly: Signior Lucio,
    did not you say you knew that Friar Lodowick to be 20
    a dishonest person?

LUCIO: *Cucullus non facit monachum,* honest in nothing but
    in his clothes, and one that hath spoke most villainous
    speeches of the Duke.

ESCALUS: We shall entreat you to abide here till he come, 25
    and enforce them against him: we shall find this Friar a
    notable fellow.

LUCIO: As any in Vienna, on my word.

ESCALUS: Call that same Isabel here once again, I would
    speak with her: Pray you, my Lord, give me leave to 30
    question, you shall see how I'll handle her.

LUCIO: Not better than he, by her own report.

ESCALUS: Say you?

LUCIO: Marry sir, I think if you handled her privately she
would sooner confess, perchance publicly she'll be
asham'd.

Enter Duke (as Friar), Provost, Isabella.

5 ESCALUS: I will go darkly to work with her.

LUCIO: That's the way: for women are light at midnight.

ESCALUS: Come on Mistress, here's a Gentlewoman,
Denies all that you have said.

LUCIO: My Lord, here comes the rascal I spoke of, here,
10 with the Provost.

ESCALUS: In very good time: Speak not you to him, till
we call upon you.

LUCIO: Mum.

ESCALUS: Come, Sir, did you set these women on to
15 slander Lord Angelo? they have confess'd you did.

DUKE: 'Tis false.

ESCALUS: How? Know you where you are?

DUKE: Respect to your great place; and let the devil
Be sometime honour'd for his burning throne.
20 Where is the Duke? 'tis he should hear me speak.

ESCALUS: The Duke's in us: and we will hear you speak,
Look you speak justly.

DUKE: Boldly, at least. But oh poor souls,
Come you to seek the Lamb here of the Fox;
25 Good night to your redress: Is the Duke gone?
Then is your cause gone too: The Duke's unjust,
Thus to retort your manifest appeal,
And put your trial in the villain's mouth,
Which here you come to accuse.

30 LUCIO: This is the rascal: this is he I spoke of.

ESCALUS: Why, thou unreverend, and unhallowed Friar:
Is't not enough thou hast suborn'd these women,
To accuse this worthy man? but in foul mouth,

And in the witness of his proper ear,
To call him villain: and then to glance from him,
To th' Duke himself, to tax him with injustice?
Take him hence; to th' rack with him: we'll touse you
Joint by joint, but we will know his purpose: 5
What? unjust?

DUKE: Be not so hot: the Duke
Dare no more stretch this finger of mine, than he
Dare rack his own: his subject am I not,
Nor here provincial: My business in this State   10
Made me a looker on here in Vienna,
Where I have seen corruption boil and bubble,
Till it o'errun the stew: Laws, for all faults,
But faults so countenanc'd that the strong Statutes
Stand like the forfeits in a barber's shop,   15
As much in mock, as mark.

ESCALUS: Slander to th' State:
Away with him to prison.

ANGELO: What can you vouch against him Signior Lucio?
Is this the man that you did tell us of?   20

LUCIO: 'Tis he, my Lord: come hither goodman bald-
pate, do you know me?

DUKE: I remember you Sir, by the sound of your voice, I
met you at the prison, in the absence of the Duke.

LUCIO: Oh, did you so? and do you remember what you   25
said of the Duke?

DUKE: Most notedly Sir.

LUCIO: Do you so Sir: And was the Duke a flesh-monger,
a fool, and a coward, as you then reported him to
be?   30

DUKE: You must (Sir) change persons with me, ere you
make that my report: you indeed spoke so of him, and
much more, much worse.

LUCIO: Oh thou damnable fellow: did not I pluck thee
by the nose, for thy speeches?

DUKE: I protest, I love the Duke, as I love myself.

ANGELO: Hark how the villain would close now, after his
5 treasonable abuses.

ESCALUS: Such a fellow is not to be talk'd withal: Away
with him to prison: Where is the Provost? away with
him to prison: lay bolts enough upon him: let him speak
no more: away with those giglets too, and with the
10 other confederate companion.

DUKE: Stay Sir, stay awhile.

ANGELO: What, resists he? help him Lucio.

LUCIO: Come sir, come, sir, come sir: foh sir, why you
bald-pated lying rascal: you must be hooded must you?
15 show your knave's visage with a pox to you: show your
sheep-biting face, and be hang'd an hour: will't not off?

DUKE: Thou art the first knave, that e'er mad'st a Duke.
First Provost, let me bail these gentle three:
Sneak not away Sir, for the Friar, and you,
20 Must have a word anon: lay hold on him.

LUCIO: This may prove worse than hanging.

DUKE: What you have spoke, I pardon: sit you down,
We'll borrow place of him; Sir, by your leave:
Hast thou or word, or wit, or impudence,
25 That yet can do thee office? If thou hast
Rely upon it, till my tale be heard,
And hold no longer out.

ANGELO: Oh my dread Lord,
I should be guiltier than my guiltiness,
30 To think I can be undiscernible,
When I perceive your grace, like power divine,
Hath look'd upon my passes. Then good Prince,
No longer session hold upon my shame,

But let my trial, be mine own confession:
Immediate sentence then, and sequent death,
Is all the grace I beg.

DUKE: Come hither Mariana,
Say: wast thou e'er contracted to this woman? 5

ANGELO: I was my Lord.

DUKE: Go take her hence, and marry her instantly.
Do you the office (Friar) which consummate,
Return him here again: go with him, Provost.

Exeunt Angelo, Mariana, Friar Peter and Provost. 10

ESCALUS: My Lord, I am more amaz'd at his dishonour,
Than at the strangeness of it.

DUKE: Come hither Isabel,
Your Friar is now your Prince: As I was then
Advertising, and holy to your business, 15
(Not changing heart with habit) I am still,
Attorneyed at your service.

ISABELLA: Oh give me pardon
That I, your vassal, have employ'd and pain'd
Your unknown sovereignty. 20

DUKE: You are pardon'd Isabel:
And now, dear Maid, be you as free to us.
Your brother's death I know sits at your heart:
And you may marvel, why I obscur'd myself,
Labouring to save his life: and would not rather 25
Make rash remonstrance of my hidden power,
Than let him so be lost: Oh most kind Maid,
It was the swift celerity of his death,
Which I did think, with slower foot came on,
That brain'd my purpose: but peace be with him, 30
That life is better life past fearing death,
Than that which lives to fear: make it your comfort,
So happy is your brother.

Enter Angelo, Mariana, Peter, Provost.

ISABELLA: I do, my Lord.

DUKE: For this new-married man approaching here,
Whose salt imagination yet hath wrong'd
5   Your well defended honour: you must pardon
For Mariana's sake: But as he adjudg'd your brother,
Being criminal, in double violation
Of sacred chastity, and of promise-breach,
Thereon dependent for your brother's life,
10 The very mercy of the Law cries out
Most audible, even from his proper tongue,
An Angelo for Claudio, death for death:
Haste still pays haste, and leisure, answers leisure;
Like doth quit like, and *Measure* still for *Measure*:
15 Then, Angelo, thy fault's thus manifested;
Which though thou wouldst deny, denies thee vantage.
We do condemn thee to the very block
Where Claudio stoop'd to death, and with like haste.
Away with him.

20 MARIANA: Oh my most gracious Lord,
I hope you will not mock me with a husband?

DUKE: It is your husband mock'd you with a husband,
Consenting to the safeguard of your honour,
I thought your marriage fit: else imputation,
25 For that he knew you, might reproach your life,
And choke your good to come: For his possessions,
Although by confiscation they are ours;
We do instate, and widow you withal,
To buy you a better husband.

30 MARIANA: Oh my dear Lord,
I crave no other, nor no better man.

DUKE: Never crave him, we are definitive.

MARIANA: Gentle my Liege.

DUKE: You do but lose your labour. Away with him to
   death: Now Sir, to you.
MARIANA: Oh my good Lord; sweet Isabel, take my part,
   Lend me your knees, and all my life to come,
   I'll lend you all my life to do you service.   5
DUKE: Against all sense you do importune her,
   Should she kneel down, in mercy of this fact,
   Her brother's ghost, his paved bed would break,
   And take her hence in horror.
MARIANA: Isabel: 10
   Sweet Isabel, do yet but kneel by me,
   Hold up your hands, say nothing: I'll speak all.
   They say best men are moulded out of faults,
   And, for the most, become much more the better
   For being a little bad: So may my husband.   15
   Oh Isabel: will you not lend a knee?
DUKE: He dies for Claudio's death.
ISABELLA: Most bounteous Sir,
   Look if it please you, on this man condemn'd,
   As if my brother liv'd: I partly think,   20
   A due sincerity governed his deeds,
   Till he did look on me: Since it is so,
   Let him not die: my brother had but justice,
   In that he did the thing for which he died.
   For Angelo, his act did not o'ertake his bad intent,   25
   And must be buried but as an intent
   That perish'd by the way: thoughts are no subjects,
   Intents, but merely thoughts.
MARIANA: Merely my Lord.
DUKE: Your suit's unprofitable: stand up I say: 30
   I have bethought me of another fault.
   Provost, how came it Claudio was beheaded
   At an unusual hour?

PROVOST: It was commanded so.

DUKE: Had you a special warrant for the deed?

PROVOST: No my good Lord: it was by private message.

DUKE: For which I do discharge you of your office,
5   Give up your keys.

PROVOST: Pardon me, noble Lord.
      I thought it was a fault, but knew it not,
      Yet did repent me after more advice,
      For testimony whereof, one in the prison
10   That should by private order else have died,
      I have reserv'd alive.

DUKE: What's he?

PROVOST: His name is Barnardine.

DUKE: I would thou hadst done so by Claudio:
15   Go fetch him hither, let me look upon him.
                        Exit Provost.

ESCALUS: I am sorry, one so learned, and so wise
      As you, Lord Angelo, have still appear'd
      Should slip so grossly, both in the heat of blood
20   And lack of temper'd judgement afterward.

ANGELO: I am sorry, that such sorrow I procure,
      And so deep sticks it in my penitent heart,
      That I crave death more willingly than mercy,
      'Tis my deserving, and I do entreat it.

25   *Enter Barnardine and Provost, Claudio (muffled),*
                        Julietta.

DUKE: Which is that Barnardine?

PROVOST: This my Lord.

DUKE: There was a Friar told me of this man.
30   Sirrah, thou art said to have a stubborn soul
      That apprehends no further than this world,
      And squar'st thy life according: Thou'rt condemn'd.
      But for those earthly faults, I quit them all,

And pray thee take this mercy to provide
For better times to come: Friar advise him,
I leave him to your hand. What muffled fellow's that?
PROVOST: This is another prisoner that I sav'd,
 Who should have died when Claudio lost his head, 5
 As like almost to Claudio, as himself.
    Unmuffles Claudio.
DUKE: If he be like your brother, for his sake
 Is he pardon'd, and for your lovely sake
 Give me your hand, and say you will be mine, 10
 He is my brother too: But fitter time for that:
 By this Lord Angelo perceives he's safe,
 Methinks I see a quickning in his eye:
 Well Angelo, your evil quits you well.
 Look that you love your wife her worth, worth yours. 15
 I find an apt remission in myself:
 And yet here's one in place I cannot pardon,
 You sirrah, that knew me for a fool, a coward,
 One all of luxury, an ass, a madman:
 Wherein have I so deserv'd of you 20
 That you extol me thus?
LUCIO: 'Faith my Lord, I spoke it but according to the
 trick: if you will hang me for it you may: but I had
 rather it would please you, I might be whipp'd.
DUKE: Whipp'd first, sir, and hang'd after. 25
 Proclaim it Provost round about the City,
 If any woman wrong'd by this lewd fellow
 (As I have heard him swear himself there's one
 Whom he begot with child) let her appear,
 And he shall marry her: the nuptial finish'd, 30
 Let him be whipp'd and hang'd.
LUCIO: I beseech your Highness do not marry me to a
 whore: your Highness said even now I made you a

Duke, good my Lord, do not recompense me, in making
me a cuckold.

DUKE: Upon mine honour thou shalt marry her.
Thy slanders I forgive, and therewithal
5 Remit thy other forfeits: take him to prison,
And see our pleasure herein executed.

LUCIO: Marrying a punk my Lord, is pressing to death,
whipping and hanging.

DUKE: Slandering a Prince deserves it.
10 She Claudio that you wrong'd, look you restore.
Joy to you Mariana, love her Angelo:
I have confess'd her, and I know her virtue.
Thanks good friend, Escalus, for thy much goodness,
There's more behind that is more gratulate.
15 Thanks Provost for thy care, and secrecy,
We shall employ thee in a worthier place.
Forgive him Angelo, that brought you home
The head of Ragozine for Claudio's,
The offence pardons itself. Dear Isabel,
20 I have a motion much imports your good,
Whereto if you'll a willing ear incline;
What's mine is yours, and what is yours is mine.
So bring us to our Palace, where we'll show
What's yet behind, that's meet you all should know.
25   *Exeunt.*

NOTES

References are to the page and line of this edition;
there are 33 lines to a full page.

THE ACTORS' NAMES: The list is given at the end P. 20
of the Folio text.

Of government . . . discourse: it were mere affectation P. 21 LL. 5–6
for me to make a speech about the principles of
government.

is able: A sentence seems to have been omitted. P. 21 L. 10

commission: document formally confirming the ap- P. 21 L. 15
pointment.

deputation: appointment as Deputy. P. 21 L. 22

can . . . advertise: teach me how to govern. P. 22 L. 16

mortality: power of life and death. P. 22 L. 19

I love . . . vehement: A remark which would have P. 23
appealed to James I who, unlike his predecessor LL. 12–15
Queen Elizabeth I, disliked cheering crowds.

look . . . bottom: examine carefully. P. 23 L. 24

Grace is grace: with a pun on *grace*: holy life. P. 24 L. 26

shears . . . us: i.e., we were cut from the same piece P. 24
of cloth. LL. 29–30

lists: outer edge or useless selvedge made of plain P. 24 L. 31
material in weaving.

three-pil'd . . . velvet: the richest kind of thick velvet P. 25 LL. 2–4
– with a pun on *piled*: bald – the result of venereal
disease.

French crown: the same joke as above; as Bottom P. 25 L. 21
observed, 'Some of your French crowns have no
hair at all.'

houses: brothels. In Shakespeare's London the P. 26 L. 30
brothels were situated in the suburbs north and south
of the city.

P. 27 L. 27 *by weight:* heavily.

P. 28 L. 20 *look'd after:* seriously regarded.

P. 28 L. 21 *contract:* betrothal. Formal betrothal was regarded as a binding contract of marriage.

P. 28 L. 29 *made them:* i.e., our friends.

P. 29 L. 2 *fault ... newness:* mistaken glamour.

P. 30 LL. 1–2 *tick-tack:* a game played on a board with pegs set into holes.

P. 30 L. 10 *dribbling dart:* arrow feebly shot.

P. 31 L. 6 *dead to infliction:* i.e., which have become a dead letter.

P. 31 L. 22 *in th' ambush:* under cover.

P. 32 L. 2 *If ... seemers:* if power changes its nature from what it seems to be.

P. 32 L. 10 *Votarists of St Clare:* The Order of St Clare was founded by St Francis of Assisi in 1212. The nuns followed strict rules and gave themselves to meditation and educating the young.

P. 32 L. 15 *Turn ... key:* used both of locking and unlocking a door: here 'unlocking'.

P. 33 L. 9 *lapwing:* a bird which leads intruders away from the nest by pretending to be injured; so, a deceiver.

P. 33 LL. 30–1 *Bore ... in hand:* deceived.

P. 34 L. 33 *As ... them:* as if they possessed (*owed*) them, i.e., the right of granting.

P. 36 L. 13 *nothing ... partial:* no partiality be shown to me.

P. 36 L. 25 *brakes of ice:* an unusual phrase, perhaps corrupt. *brakes:* thickets. *answer none:* are never called to account.

P. 36 L. 26 *fault alone:* single lapse.

P. 37 L. 16 *parcel bawd:* partly bawd, partly tapster.

P. 37 LL. 18–19 *professes a hothouse:* owns a brothel.

P. 37 L. 21 *detest:* for protest.

misplaces: misuses words – like so many of Shake- P. 38 L. 6
speare's under-educated characters.

Bunch of Grapes: the name of a room in the house. P. 39 LL. 10–11

suppos'd: for deposed, sworn as a witness. P. 40 L. 4

respected: for suspected. P. 40 L. 11

let . . . brother: i.e., condemn the fault but forgive the P. 45 LL. 26–7
sinner.

cipher . . . function: an officer worth nothing. P. 45 L. 31

fine . . . record: to punish faults that are already con- P. 45 L. 32
demned.

had . . . brother: i.e., he is as good as dead. P. 46 L. 2

And . . . took: i.e., Christ who might have taken his P. 47 L. 6
opportunity to punish.

glass: a magic glass which foretells the future. P. 47 L. 31

successive degrees: successors. P. 48 L. 1

glassy essence: fragile nature. P. 48 L. 25

spleens: The spleen was regarded as the seat of P. 48 L. 27
laughter.

laugh mortal: laugh themselves to death. P. 48 L. 28

skins . . . top: covers the sore but does not cure it. P. 49 L. 9

cross: are at cross purposes. P. 50 L. 4

but . . . season: i.e., the same sun which brings the P. 50
violet to sweetness causes the carrion body to stink. LL. 13–16

blister'd her report: blemished her reputation. P. 51 L. 18

As that: because. P. 52 L. 10

we . . . fear: i.e., avoid displeasing God not because P. 52
we love Him but because we fear Him. LL. 12–13

fear'd: the Folio reading. Some editors emend to P. 53 L. 5
sear'd: withered.

idle plume: useless feather – the outward mark of a P. 53 L. 7
brainless gallant.

general subject: common crowd. See note on p. 23 P. 53 L. 24
ll. 12–15.

know: Angelo cynically sees a double meaning in P. 53 L. 30
'know your pleasure' – have carnal knowledge.

P. 54 L. 6   *fitted :* prepared for death.

P. 54 L. 12   *stamps :* lit., the dies from which coins are struck.

P. 54   *Falsely . . . one :* i.e., it is much the same to take away
LL. 13–15 the life of a man lawfully begotten as to create an
          illegitimate child (lit., to make a false coin by using
          metal in a forbidden way).

P. 54   *our . . . accompt :* sins we are forced to commit are
LL. 24–5 counted but not charged up against us.

P. 54 L. 33   *Please you :* if you were willing.

P. 55   *As . . . question :* as I do not admit that or anything
LL. 26–7 else but for the sake of the argument.

P. 55 L. 31   *all-building :* the Folio reading. Theobald's con-
          jecture of 'all-binding' may be correct.

P. 56 L. 16   *Ignomy in ransom :* a disgraceful payment for release.

P. 56   *Else . . . weakness :* a difficult passage, probably cor-
LL. 28–30 rupt. *feodary :* confederate. *owe :* own.

P. 57 L. 2   *profiting by :* taking advantage of.

P. 57 L. 4   *credulous . . . prints :* deceived by false impressions.

P. 57 L. 9   *arrest . . . words :* take you at your word.

P. 57 L. 13   *destin'd livery :* i.e., natural frailty of your sex. *livery :*
          lit., the uniform worn by a servant.

P. 59 L. 10   *skyey :* heavenly, of the stars, so fated.

P. 59   *fork . . . worm :* the snake (*worm*) was believed to
LL. 17–18 sting with its forked tongue.

P. 59 L. 25   *complexion . . . effects :* your natural intention is con-
          tinually varying. Man, it was believed, was made up
          of four humours – earth, air, fire, and water. If any
          one humour predominated, his nature became un-
          balanced, and the predominating humour was re-
          vealed in his outward appearance (*complexion*).

P. 60 LL. 5–6 *alms . . . eld :* charity for a paralysed old man.

P. 61 L. 1   *Leiger :* a resident ambassador, as distinguished from
          an Ambassador Extraordinary sent on a special mis-
          sion.

P. 61 L. 15   *determin'd scope :* fixed limits.

P. 61 L. 20   *point :* i.e., truth.

In base appliances: by low means.   P. 62 L. 5

prenzie . . . prenzie: A much annotated word. In the first use it apparently means Deputy (*principe*): the second may be a printer's error caught up from the previous use; it requires a meaning of 'respectable, hypocritical'.   P. 62 LL. 11–14

in cold obstruction: stiff and cold.   P. 63 L. 8

sensible . . . clod: conscious warm body to become trodden earth.   P. 63 LL. 9–10

warped . . . wilderness: degenerate throwback.   P. 63 L. 33

practise his judgement: experiment.   P. 64 L. 22

satisfy . . . resolution: find your certainty; i.e., deceive yourself with false hopes.   P. 64 LL. 26–7

resolve him: give him my answer.   P. 65 L. 16

discover his government: reveal his misgovernment.   P. 65 LL. 20–1

in few . . . lamentation: briefly, he left her to her own grief.   P. 66 LL. 19–20

refer . . . advantage: demand for yourself this condition.   P. 67 L. 3

stead . . . appointment: keep the appointment yourself.   P. 67 LL. 7–8

scaled: weighed, found wanting.   P. 67 L. 12

moated grange: large farm surrounded by a moat.   P. 67 L. 21

bastard: lit., a sweet Spanish wine.   P. 67 L. 31

two usuries: i.e., prostitution and money-lending.   P. 67 L. 33

furr'd gown: a gown trimmed with fur, worn by prosperous merchants. It is often used as the symbol of wealth gained by dishonest means.   P. 68 L. 2

craft . . . facing: cunning is symbolized by the fur trimming.   P. 68 LL. 3–4

stinkingly depending: depending on such a stinking support.   P. 68 L. 20

mile . . . errand: make a fruitless journey.   P. 68 L. 30

clutch'd: i.e., full of money.   P. 69 L. 8

Trot: a contemptuous phrase, usually applied to an old woman.   P. 69 L. 10

P. 69 L. 17   *tub:* pickle tub, used as a hot bath for the cure of venereal disease.

P. 70 L. 1   *mettle:* with a pun on *metal,* i.e., irons.

P. 71 LL. 3–4 *motion generative:* masculine puppet.

P. 71 L. 7   *rebellion . . . codpiece:* i.e., because he was overcome by lust. The codpiece was the opening in front of the hose.

P. 71 L. 18   *clack-dish:* the wooden bowl of the professional beggar.

P. 71 L. 27   *file:* number; lit., list. *subject:* people.

P. 71 L. 32   *warranted need:* if assurance is required.

P. 73 LL. 2   *mutton on Fridays:* lit., no fasting man. Mutton also means a prostitute.

P. 73 L. 23   *Philip and Jacob:* The day of SS Philip and James is May 1st.

P. 73 L. 30   *wrought . . . pity:* acted as mercifully as I would.

P. 74 L. 33   *paid . . . function:* done your duty to God.

P. 75 L. 1   *debt . . . calling:* what your holy office requires.

P. 75 L. 11   *He who:* This passage in rhymed octosyllabic verse is regarded by some critics as not written by Shakespeare; but there is no reason to doubt its genuineness, for the little sermon is quite in keeping with the Duke-Friar's character. A change of metre from the freer blank verse to the stiffness of this rhyme emphasizes its gnomic nature.

P. 77 L. 13   *In . . . precept:* instructing me by the gesture.

P. 77 L. 16   *concerning . . . observance:* which she must observe.

P. 79 LL. 30–1 *favour:* (1) kindness (2) face.

P. 79 L. 32   *occupation:* trade, manual work.

P. 80 L. 17   *ask forgiveness:* It was part of the etiquette of an execution for the hangman to ask for the forgiveness of his victim.

P. 81 LL. 1–2 *As . . . bones:* i.e., like the innocent sleep that comes to the weary traveller.

P. 81 L. 32   *unsisting:* the Folio reading. The word is otherwise unknown and is variously emended – unresisting, unassisting, etc.

desperately mortal: in a state of desperate mortal sin. P. 83 L. 29

unfolding Star: the morning star which calls the shep- P. 85 L. 17
herd to lead his sheep from the sheepfold.

present shrift: immediate absolution – i.e., prepara- P. 85 L. 21
tion for death.

commodity ... dead: Interest on loans had been fixed P. 86 LL. 1–4
at 10 per cent, but money-lenders evaded the statute
by the legal device of 'commodities'. In return for
a loan of cash the borrower also purchased a parcel
(*commodity*) of worthless goods, such as lutestrings,
for which he promised to pay a much higher sum.
Master Rash's 'commodity' consisted of brown
paper and ginger.

rapier and dagger man: i.e., bully. P. 86 LL. 9–10

Shooty: i.e., shoe-tie. P. 86 L. 12

for the Lord's sake: Prisoners were obliged to pay for P. 86 L. 14
their own food in prison. Those who had no money
were allowed to appeal for the charity of passers-by
to give them alms 'for the Lord's sake'.

under generation: i.e., the Antipodes. P. 88 L. 24

free dependant: entirely your servant. P. 88 L. 26

cold gradation: deliberate progress. P. 89 L. 3

men of sort and suit: persons of rank and petitioners. P. 92 L. 13

veil ... purpose: conceal our full plan. P. 93 L. 25

Forerunning ... requital: preceding other kinds of P. 94 L. 25
reward.

wards ... bosom: secrets of my heart. P. 94 L. 28

the subject: my subjects. P. 95 L. 1

vail your regard: lower your glance. P. 95 L. 9

to the matter: i.e., fitting. P. 97 L. 30

seal'd in approbation: warranted as true. P. 102 L. 33

Cucullus ... monachum: a cowl does not make a P. 103 L. 22
monk.

forfeits ... barber's shop: teeth extracted by barbers P. 105 L. 15
(who were also surgeons and dentists), strung up as
trophies of their trade.

P. 105 L. 16　*as . . . mark:* to be mocked at as much as to be observed.

P. 107 L. 26　*rash remonstrance:* hasty demonstration.

P. 108 L. 28　*widow . . . withal:* bestow on you as his widow.

P. 109 L. 8　*paved:* Persons of rank were buried inside the church underneath the pavement.

P. 109 L. 25　*act . . . intent:* did not actually commit the act which he intended.

P. 111 L. 16　*remission:* readiness to forgive.

P. 112 L. 7　*pressing to death:* Accused persons who refused to plead at trial in a court of law were condemned to be pressed to death under a weighted board.

P. 112 L. 12　*confess'd:* heard her confession (when posing as a Friar).

GLOSSARY

absolute : perfect
absolute for : certain of
accommodation : comfort
accountant : forfeit
advertising : attentive
affect : desire
affection : (*a*) lust (*b*) feeling
after : (*a*) like (*b*) at the rate of
Allhallond eve : Halloween
apace : excessively
appointment : preparation
approbation : noviciate
approof : approval
attorneyed : employed as pleader
avis'd : aware

bane : poison
bay : window
bear : behave
behind : to come
blench : start aside
blood : passions
bonds : obligation
boot : advantage
borne up : planned
bosom : heart, desire
bowels : i.e., children
bravery : ostentation
breeds : quickens, stirs
bringings forth : actions
by and by : at once

caitiff : wretch

case : outside
censured : passed judgement on
ceremony : symbol of greatness
character : (*a*) letter (*b*) handwriting (*c*) mark of distinction
close : secret
close : climb down
combinate : affianced
combined : bound
compact : confederate
composition : agreement
compound : come to terms
concupiscible : lecherous
countenance : favouritism
covent : convent
crotchets : odd ways
cross : thwart
custom shrunk : without customers

definitive : resolute
deliberate : severe
depose : give evidence
determin'd : decided
devices : plots
dispenses with : absolves
dissolution : death
disvouch'd : contradicted
dressings : outward shows
drift : purpose

enforce : declare

enroll'd: statutory
enshield: concealed
enskied: heavenly
estimation: worth
events: affairs

fact: deed, crime
fall: let fall
fear: frighten
fewness: in brief
figure: likeness
flaws: gusts of passion
flourish: embellish
foison: plenty
fond: foolish, doting
foppery: folly
force: enforce, rape
forfeit: offending
forted: fortified
frame: purpose
friend: mistress

generous: well born
giglets: wantons
gratulate: gratify
gravel: stony
gyves: fetters

Hallowmas: All Saints' Day, November 1st
happily: perhaps
head: face
head (vb): behead
helmed: steered
hent: occupied
hold: observe
husband: housekeeper

image: thought
imputation: slander
inequality: injustice
informal: crazy
instruction: spiritual advice
invention: imagination

jade: horse of feeble spirit
journal: daily

leaven'd: allowed to work like leaven, matured
liberty: licentiousness
limit: appointed time
limited: appointed
lists: limits
luxury: lust

maw: stomach
meal'd: spotted
merely: entirely
metal: material, worth
moe: more
mortality: human life
motion: proposal
mouth (vb): kiss

organs: instruments

pace: direct
pain: penalty
passes: trespasses
peculiar: private
pelting: paltry
perfect: fully inform
persuasion: information
pick-lock: skeleton key

pilgrimage : i.e., earthly life

pin : trifle

pith : main purpose

planched : planked

poise : weight

powder'd : pickled, steeped in brine

practice : plot

precise : puritanical

pregnant : expert, obvious

present : immediate

probation : (a) proof (b) noviciate

proclamation : public report

prolixious : superfluous, unnecessary

prone : affection

propagation : increase

proper : own

proportion : metre

proportions : possessions, dowry

put : made

put in : make a bid

putting on : urging

qualify : moderate

quests : inquiries

quit : pay back, pay for, forgive

rack : stretch out, pull to pieces

ravin : devour greedily

rebate : dull

remit : pardon

remorse : pity

repell'd : refused

respected : suspected

restraint : arrest

retort : reject

rheum : excess of moisture causing rheumatism

salt : lustful

science : expert knowledge

scope : liberty

scruple : minute part, hesitation

sense : meaning, intention

serpigo : a skin disease

settled : firm, solemn

sheep-biting : sheep-stealing

shore : limit

sicles : shekels

siege : seat

sinister : unjust

sith : since

snatches : wisecracks

splay : castrate

square : measure

stead : help

steel'd : hard-hearted

still : always

story : theme for scandal

suborn'd : bribed to accuse

sufferance : suffering

surfeiting : growing sick with excess

sweat : sweating sickness, the plague

tax : censure, charge

temporary : in temporal matters

tender : offer

terms : law terms

thrilling : freezing

tickle : unsteady

tie: trim short
tilter: fencer
touch'd: tested
tundish: funnel

ungenitur'd: impotent
ungot: unbegotten
usurp: falsely assume

vastidity: immensity

viewless: unseen
vouch: declaration

warp: deviate
weary: wearisome
well-seeming: hypocritical
wreakless: reckless

yare: handy

zodiacs: years

PENGUIN POPULAR CLASSICS

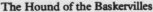

Published or forthcoming

Aesop	Aesop's Fables
Hans Andersen	Fairy Tales
Louisa May Alcott	Good Wives
	Little Women
Eleanor Atkinson	Greyfriars Bobby
Jane Austen	Emma
	Mansfield Park
	Northanger Abbey
	Persuasion
	Pride and Prejudice
	Sense and Sensibility
R. M. Ballantyne	The Coral Island
J. M. Barrie	Peter Pan
Frank L. Baum	The Wonderful Wizard of Oz
Anne Brontë	Agnes Grey
	The Tenant of Wildfell Hall
Charlotte Brontë	Jane Eyre
	The Professor
	Shirley
	Villette
Emily Brontë	Wuthering Heights
John Buchan	Greenmantle
	The Thirty-Nine Steps
Frances Hodgson Burnett	A Little Princess
	Little Lord Fauntleroy
	The Secret Garden
Samuel Butler	The Way of All Flesh
Lewis Carroll	Alice's Adventures in Wonderland
	Through the Looking Glass
Geoffrey Chaucer	The Canterbury Tales
G. K. Chesterton	Father Brown Stories
Erskine Childers	The Riddle of the Sands
John Cleland	Fanny Hill
Wilkie Collins	The Moonstone
	The Woman in White
Sir Arthur Conan Doyle	The Adventures of Sherlock Holmes
	His Last Bow
	The Hound of the Baskervilles

PENGUIN POPULAR CLASSICS

Published or forthcoming

PENGUIN POPULAR POETRY